About the Author

Maya Sharma is a 11th grade student at Eastside Preparatory School in Washington State. She has won several prizes in science, math, essay writing, and arts at school, state, and national competitions. Maya loves to travel globally, read books, play piano, and spend time with her friends. Maya has been writing for her school newsletter since 4th grade. She has tackled the topics of technology, automation, diversity, politics, and gender equality in her columns. She won first place in a state-wide essay competition organized by World Affairs Council. Her essay on "Strategies and Solutions to solve the Global Water Crisis" focused on strategies that every community can embrace. She is the captain of her school's robotics team.

D1546137

Paving
Conversations with Incredible Women Who are Shaping our World

Maya Sharma

Paving
Conversations with Incredible
Women who are Shaping our World

Olympia Publishers
London

www.olympiapublishers.com
OLYMPIA PAPERBACK EDITION

A CIP catalogue record for this title is
available from the British Library.

ISBN: 978-1-78830-710-9

Every effort has been made to trace copyright holders and to obtain
their permission for the use of copyright material. The publisher
apologises for any errors or omissions in the above list and would
be grateful if notified of any corrections that should be incorporated
in future reprints or editions of this book

First Published in 2021

Olympia Publishers
Tallis House
2 Tallis Street
London
EC4Y 0AB
Printed in Great Britain

Dedication

Dedicated to my mom who is my role model and has paved the way for me.

Acknowledgements

This book is a dream come true.

It started out as a prodded curiosity and blossomed into a life changing journey. If participating in the historic women's march in 2017 gave me a nudge to explore my world view, then the interview with my hometown mayor on a drizzly cold day in a local coffee shop gave me my purpose for this sojourn. Over the next 18 months, one step at a time, one interview after another, I was fortunate to converse with some of the most amazing women on the planet. Their accomplishments inspired me; their humbleness and encouragement let me dream big, and the result is in your hands.

I am forever indebted for their time and pearls of wisdom.

None of this would have been possible without the help of scores of angels who stepped in to provide the necessary nudge at the right time to keep me going. Thank you, Mary Lou Pauly for running for Mayor of Issaquah and giving me the first interview that started it all. Doing my first interview of an elected official, at age 14, was a thrilling experience. She encouraged me to reach out to other mayors, congresswomen and senators from our state, so, I did.

I am grateful to Mayor of Seattle Jenny Durkan who is a trailblazer, Congresswoman Pramila Jayapal who has an incredible immigrant story, Senator Maria Cantwell who understands the technology world better than most politicians, and Senator Patty Murray who went from an elementary school teacher dissatisfied with the state of affairs to becoming one of the most brilliant senators of our nation. Their tireless staff members—Kamaria Hightower, Noelle Rosellini, Eric Marter, and Kerry Arndt helped squeeze my interviews into their extremely busy schedules.

Dr. Janet Yellen was so gracious with her time and her words of wisdom and encouragement. My time with her is something I will treasure for the rest of my life. My thanks to Ruth Mundy, the prime minister's assistant, whose persistence and openness provided me insights from New Zealand's prime minister, Jacinda Ardern. I am her biggest fan, so I was delighted to have a chance to ask her a few questions.

Nobel Prize winners Dr. Ada Yonath and Jody Williams reminded me why they are so brilliant; their clarity of thought is something I aspire to have. Dr. Ana Mari Cauce is president at the University of Washington — the highest rated public university in the world. She was very supportive of my endeavors and boosted my confidence in keep pushing with this book project.

Journalists Laurie Segall and Emily Chang gave me new insights into their professions. I was over the moon in conversing with astrophysicist Dr. Jocelyn Bell Burnell and astronaut Dr. Ellen Ochoa. Their inspiring stories and views of the world will inspire any kid or (adult for that matter) in the cosmos. The adventurous spirit emanating from the athletic prowess of Lindsey Vonn and Squash Falconer was infectious. I really appreciate all they do for girls like me.

The business superwomen Beth Comstock, Arianna

Huffington, Adena Friedman, and Safra Catz gave me new ideas to pursue my dreams and learn new subjects to explore my curiosity. Entrepreneurs Ann Crady Weiss, Robin Hauser, Ilana Stern, and Tiffany Pham created new businesses out of nothing and showed that anything is possible when you dream big.

As the saying goes, it takes a village.

There were many people who helped me in this journey in setting up the interviews, facilitating the introductions, and giving me a push to keep going. My thanks to Laura Kildow, Melanie Wagner, Doug Suriano, Sheri Shon, Ralph Simon, Genevieve Haas, Mitch Lewis, Monica Lee, and Om Malik for their assistance.

As I mentioned in my introduction, I started publishing these interviews in my school newsletter, The Eagle Eye at Eastside Preparatory School in Washington State in 8th grade. The process helped me in flexing my writing muscles and explore my nascent capabilities. The feedback from teachers and my friends was quite useful in getting better with each edition.

One of the people who played an important role in my journey in finishing this book was Ashley Parker, the Pulitzer Prize winning journalist at The Washington Post. She was not only so gracious with her time—despite her insane schedule of covering the White House in Washington DC (I know!)—she encouraged me and helped me whenever I needed it. She has been an amazing role model for me. Ashley, I live by your words every day. I can't thank you enough for being such a nice friend and mentor and for penning a wonderful foreword for the book.

Many people claim to be for girls' advancement and

promoting equal opportunity. These extraordinary folks are living it by doing it, quietly, behind the scenes.

My thanks also to James Houghton at Olympia Publishers for taking a chance on a first-time author from high school.

Finally, to my mom and dad, thanks a zillion. Thank you for being my very own pair of wonder parents! I am thankful for all your support to help me get through this project during my busy high school years. I love you both so much! My mischievous little brother Anish gave me fresh ideas for questions and interview candidates. I hope you write your own tome one day that paves the way for others.

As I said, it was a team effort.

To all the young girls out there, you are the reason why I wanted to write this book. I was learning so much from my interviews that I wanted to share it with a larger audience. I hope after reading this book, you realize that you are capable of anything, no matter what anyone tells you!

Pursue your dreams and help shape the world to be a better place for us all.

You are all Wonder Women!

Contents

Foreword

I first "met" Maya when she reached out to me, over email, for an interview for her "Paving" project. I can't remember exactly how long it took us to connect, but I know it was a while. She had to follow up once or twice; go through the Washington Post PR machine; and then we had to find a time that worked with her homework schedule and my White House responsibilities. Like I said, it took a while. And throughout it all, Maya was patient yet persistent.

When she finally called me and I heard her voice, I remember noticing both how distant she sounded, and how young. She was distant — Washington State to Washington, DC — and she was young, just 14 years old. But I also remember being impressed by her poise and the confidence with which she explained her project. Her questions were thorough and thoughtful, and she seemed to know what she wanted out of the interview. I believe it was she, not I, who initiated the call's conclusion.

When I asked her offhand with who else she had spoken to, I was also impressed. If you look at her conversations, she had interviewed both her states' senators, and her hometown mayor — not just an interview, but the first interview Issaquah

Mayor Mary Lou Pauly ever did as mayor. She had managed to cajole athletes (Olympian Lindsey Vonn), chief executives (Safra Catz, the CEO of Oracle and Adena Friedman, CEO of NASDAQ), influencers (Arianna Huffington), not-just-one-but-two Noble Laureates (Jody Williams and Ada Yonath) and, of course, politicians and journalists.

Maya had persuaded a wide range of women to speak to her, but she hadn't stopped there. Each interview is specifically tailored to her interview subject. Some of the women give short, concise answers, others wax on. Some are practical in their answers, others philosophical. But each woman is responding to a distinct set of questions, born out of Maya's diligent and exhaustive research to prepare for each interview. Yes, all of the women in the book are quite impressive, but their answers are so fascinating because Maya's questions are thoughtful and inquisitive, drawing them out.

After Maya and I spoke, I admittedly largely forgot about her book. I was busy covering the White House for the Washington Post, and then shortly after, I gave birth to a daughter. And yet, one day, I received another email from Maya; she had noticed I was going to be speaking at the CrossCut Festival in Seattle, not far from where she lives, and she wondered if we might meet after my panel.

We exchanged numbers again, and I said I'd text her as soon as I was done speaking and, hopefully, we could connect. But I didn't even have time to ping her. As soon as my panel — on covering the Donald J. Trump White House — concluded, while the lights were still dim, Maya made her way toward the stage. She was practically the first one there — again, persistent, yet waiting patiently — and she told me she'd left early from a panel by the famous musician Macklemore and, Seahawks football legend, Doug Baldwin to come hear to the political one.

We chatted a bit, and she asked me to write this foreword. Of course, I said yes. But even then, Maya wasn't finished. When I got back home, I had emails waiting from her. She gave me a deadline, and a word count. She doggedly followed up when I hadn't responded after a few days. She asked my advice on reaching several other women she hoped to include and hoped to round out her book accordingly. Again, Maya was concerned not just that she tapped impressive women, but that she was capturing a diverse group, in a range of categories.

I love that Maya considers herself a feminist. I love that she was inspired by other women, all marching together. And I love that while, initially, it was her dad pushing her, it is now Maya pushing herself and others, actively seeking out women who she's inspired by, fascinated with, curious about and interviewing them to pass on that knowledge to others in a book.

Maya calls her book subjects "Wonder Women." And she, too, is a wonder woman.

Ashley Parker
The Washington Post

Introduction

I have always been a feminist.

I have always believed women are equal to men.

I have always questioned the ignorant belief that women are less intelligent and capable than men.

I have always wanted to make change in the world.

Sitting in my chair at my desk with a terrible posture and dim lighting, for a project, I scroll through the latest articles of women being poorly treated in Eastern Europe. I keep asking myself over and over again, "Why?".

I never quite found a way to express my feelings for this until one fine morning in 2017.

January 21st, 2017. A Saturday.

My dad had told me two or three days prior to the 21st that there was going to be a Women's March. Though I truly supported the causes, I was never quite fond of marches.

"I have too much homework, I don't want to go." I repeated to my dad.

But, the next day, he somehow convinced me and we drove to Seattle. It was a very cloudy day, as it always is in Seattle during the winters. Bundled up in layers of clothes and warm garments, we walked to the march. Since we had never done a march before, we just jumped in the middle of the march to the Space Needle, Seattle's iconic landmark.

And we started walking.

I was wowed.

I was amazed.

I couldn't believe what I was seeing.

I know that when people have a passion for things, they do whatever it takes to get there, but honestly, I had never seen anything like what I was seeing that day. All around me, men, women, children, friends, and even the people that worked inside the nearby stores, had come out on a cold Saturday to this Women's March.

Big signs and banners encompassed me.

"No one is free when others are oppressed," one of the signs read.

"Respect our existence or expect our resistance," another read.

"Hear me roar," was one of my favorites.

No words, picture, video, or sign will ever be able to represent what I felt that day. We made our way through the crowd of 175,000 people.

Yes, that's right. 175,000 people.

So, as you can tell, I was quite amazed by this crowd.

However, I still kind of wanted to be at home on my chair "working" on my homework.

But then the wave came.

Not the wave that you see at football, basketball, or baseball games. But the screaming wave. It started in the back of the parade, and a few minutes later people only a few feet behind me were screaming. I freaked out thinking somebody was hurt, but as I turned around, I saw smiles on their faces. On all of their faces. Then, the people that were right on my tail were screaming as well.

I turned right, people were screaming. I turned left, people were screaming.

I didn't know what to think of it, but I did not scream. I looked up at my mom — who had also come — she was smiling.

She did not scream, but she was smiling. She saw my face and started laughing.

"What was that?" I asked her.

"I have absolutely no clue," she responded.

I looked at my brother who had the same reaction as me. Confused.

'Whatever that was, I have got to join it the next time', I thought to myself. Within a matter of minutes, I started hearing the scream wave again.

When the wave of screams got to me, I screamed.

But it wasn't a restricted scream. It wasn't that scream that you do when you get new clothes, or a Christmas present. Or the joy of your uncle or cousins coming over. It was something else.

I let all my emotions out.

Everything that I had, all the anger I had collected from reading women, mothers, and sisters being mistreated, being taken advantage of and abused because they were female. All the sadness I had jumbled up into a heavy rock of emotions that sat in the corner of my stomach, and all the happiness I had gotten from seeing all these people at the Women's March to support women; it all went into that scream. I screamed at the top of my lungs.

Slowly, one footstep after another, I was becoming more and more excited to be there.

After a few hours, my brother said, "Can we go home now? I'm hungry."

I rolled my eyes, "No, let's stay here, it's so much fun!" But, if you have younger siblings, you'll understand that they always get what they want over your wishes.

So we walked back to the car. The screams got fainter and fainter as they trailed behind us.

The next Monday, at school, I told all my friends about the women's march. I asked them if they went. I was so excited to tell everyone. It was almost like I needed to throw up the pieces of excitement in me. I apologize for the sickening metaphor. A few days later, on my way to school, my dad told me that a bunch of these women marches were held all around the nation, including at the very front steps of the White House in Washington DC.

Many months later, on one of our drives, I saw signs for the upcoming election of a new mayor in Seattle. Now, I want you to know that I don't ever pay attention to elections or politics. And I didn't pay attention to them this time either. All I remembered was that there was going to be a new mayor. A new week rolled up and my dad says, "Let's go to the mayor's debate." Without questioning him, the next day, we got there a good thirty minutes early and I was welcomed by Claude Blumenzweig—one of the three candidates running for mayor.

I ran to the front row. I sat down, my mom went to chat with a friend, my dad started scrolling through Twitter, and my brother started to read the book he had brought in anticipation of a boring debate.

I stared straight into the TV looking at the names and faces of the three candidates. Claude Blumenzweig, Paul Winterstein, and Mary Lou Pauly.

A few minutes later, Paul Winterstein showed up. And then minutes just before the Q&A session began, Mary Lou Pauly walked in with her black dress and a confident smile.

And it began: question after question.

Once again, I was bored to death, but then someone asked, "What do you plan to do with the traffic situation?" The question caught my attention as I spend a lot of time in traffic with my parents.

Both men responded by acknowledging that there is an issue with traffic in the city, but they failed to articulate their solution. Just like for many other questions, the mayoral candidates either dodged the question or gave an answer which appealed to those who funded their campaigns.

Every debate that I have seen, every speech that I have heard, every man that has stepped up on stage to win has never spoken about their solutions.

Mary Lou Pauly, however, confidently responded: she first addressed why there was even an issue in the first place then she accepted that there was a traffic problem and, lastly, she expanded on a solution. She said what she would actually do to fix the issue if she became the mayor.

Answer after answer, she gave solutions when the others passed the question on, or nervously gave answers that didn't appeal to the audience.

But Mary Lou Pauly, the only female sitting on that stage, kept on giving solutions.

Afterwards, I spoke briefly with Ms Pauly.

I left the session 100% confident that she would win.

A few days later, when the election results rolled in, Mary Lou Pauly had won with—64.19%, and Paul Winterstein—had only 35.81%.

I was glad.

Around the same time, I was writing for my school newspaper, "Eagle Eye," and I needed something to write about for the upcoming month. Previously, I had written about the school play, and on artificial intelligence.

But then an idea came to me. What if I interviewed Mayor

Lou Pauly, I asked myself?

So, I emailed her, and I got a response.

It took weeks to schedule a good time but, eventually, we worked it out.

January 1st, 2018.

Yes, that was a New Year's Day.

And not only was it the first day of 2018 and my first of many future interviews, but it was Mayor Pauly's first interview as a mayor as well: the first meeting, and first one-on-one conversation as the mayor of our city.

I remember how nervous I was the week before. I was counting down the days till the interview date.

Three days before, I had typed up my questions and printed them out.

We met at the local coffee shop.

I had never felt so happy and excited.

I mean, come on! I was interviewing the mayor!

And, as she ate her banana bread in between answers, I nervously asked her my questions and the follow-ups.

After the interview, I thanked her for the wonderful interview and I left feeling extremely relieved and proud of myself as I thought it was a pretty good first interview.

This was the start of a journey I didn't quite anticipate or plan for.

I started digging up the headlines and found more female politicians paving the way.

Jenny Durkan won the Seattle mayoral race. A first in 100 years. This led to my second interview.

I found out that both of senators from Washington were female — Maria Cantwell and Patty Murray. How awesome! They have been doing some amazing work in the senate and for our state. I familiarized myself with their policy work and requested interviews.

Seattle congresswoman Pramila Jayapal was disrupting congress as a progressive with new ideas. I even got to meet her in person at one of her constituency's town halls, and we connected. She is such a nice person.

Over the summer of 2018, after finishing school, I thought about getting a perspective from women in other domains beyond politics and got to meet some amazing women around the world — 'Wonder Women', I call them. They have paved the way for future generations through their grit, imagination, and humility. They showed the path to girls like me to dream big, never give up, never to let anyone tell you what you can and can't do, and to be resilient in the pursuit of your goals.

Each interview inspired me to do the next one. And before I knew it, I had 25 interviews from these global influencers; their stories were profound and mesmerizing. They broke barriers and paved the path for the next generation. They achieved many firsts and were destined to make a big impact on the world whether it is in science, medicine, politics, journalism, space, sports, or engineering.

So, my dear readers, the idea of the book was sparked through some serendipitous series of events. I started from politics, but expanded my purview to "women in leadership roles" and interviewed female leaders across a broad spectrum of fields from sports to economics, from adventure to journalism, from media to medicine, from science to astronomy, and much more.

It was an ambitious and daunting task for me, especially with the school work load, but with some help and persistence, I started to build my portfolio of interviews over the summer. As I was pinching myself for having the chance to talk to some of the most amazing female leaders in the world, it dawned on me that it will benefit a larger audience who might be just as curious and intrigued by the female leaders of our times as I was.

I decided that these conversations needed a bigger platform outside of the school newsletter and with enough encouragement and support, I decided to pursue the book format for my one-on-ones with these leaders who have inspired so much and so many. I feel blessed at the opportunity to talk to them and learn from their lives and worldview.

As I researched the subject and discovered some amazing women all around the world, I tried to narrow my list to represent a broad spectrum of interests, talents, and accomplishments. I wish I could have interviewed a few hundred more leaders but, for my school work, I limited them to 25. They represent some of the best and brightest in the world.

They have literally scaled the highest peaks; broken numerous glass ceilings; won Nobel and Pulitzer Prizes; ran big universities, companies, and countries; and have been an inspiration to countless men and women around the globe.

The stories of these fabulous 25 are unique: how they fought through adversity, bias, and discrimination to shine through the merits of their work and mind.

I am really proud to have these wonderful ladies contribute to my debut book and give me the encouragement to finish the project.

And so, my dear reader, I truly hope that you enjoy the interviews and draw your own lessons and inspirations.

Thanks for picking up this book. It means a lot to me.

Maya Sharma

September 2020
Seattle

With Journalist Ashley Parker (top), Congresswoman Pramila
Jayapal (bottom left), and Mayor Mary Lou Pauly (bottom right)

The Firsts

As I mentioned in my introduction, the incredible women in this book have paved the path through breaking glass ceilings and barriers, by being first in many areas. Here are some highlights:

Dr. Janet Yellen	First female Federal Reserve Chair.
Jacinda Ardern	Youngest woman in the world to lead a country.
Dr. Jocelyn Bell Burnell	First scientist to find pulsars — the most useful stars in the universe.
Pramila Jayapal	First Indian-American Congresswomen in US Congress.
Maria Cantwell	First Democrat elected to the US House of representatives from Washington's first congressional district in 40 years.
Adena Friedman	First female CEO of NASDAQ.
Safra Catz	First female CEO of Oracle.
Lindsey Vonn	First American female to win gold medal in downhill at the Winter Olympics. She won her 20th World Cup crystal global title; the overall record for men or women. She has

	the second highest super ranking of all skiers, men or women.
Dr. Ana Mari Cauce	First Cuban-born, first Latina, and first woman to serve as president of a major US university.
Dr. Ada Yonath	First Israeli Woman to win a Nobel Prize, the first woman from the middle-east to win a Nobel Prize in sciences and the first woman in 45 years to win the Nobel Prize in Chemistry that has been held by the likes of Dr Marie Curie.
Arianna Huffington	One of the first to launch a successful media company in the digital age and first female board member of Uber.
Jody Williams	For her peace efforts, she has been one of the women recognized as one of the most powerful women in the world by Forbes and Glamour magazines, in addition to dozens of honorary degrees.
Beth Comstock	First female Vice Chair of GE in its 125+ year old history.
Patty Murray	Washington state's first female senator.
Jenny Durkan	Seattle's first female mayor since the 1920s and first lesbian mayor for the city. First openly gay U.S. Attorney in country's history
Squash Falconer	First British woman to climb and paraglide from Mt. Blanc.
Dr. Ellen Ochoa	World's first Hispanic female astronaut.

Dr. Ada Yonath

Nobel Laureate in Chemistry for Work in Crystallography

Dr. Ada Yonath is an Israeli crystallographer known for her ground-breaking work on the structure of the ribosome. In 2009, Yonath was given the Nobel Prize in Chemistry for her findings on the structure and function of the ribosome. At the time, she was the first woman to win the Nobel Prize for Chemistry in 45 years. She is currently the director of the Helen and Milton A. Kimmelman center for Biomolecular Structure as well as the Assembly of Weizmann Institute of Science. Her current efforts focus on the issues of antibiotic resistance and discovering the origins of life.

Maya: *What inspired you to pursue a career in science?*
Ada: I was inspired by the process of the translation of the genetic code. I did not think about it being a career.

Maya: *What motivated you to go deeper into crystallography?*
Ada: Crystallography was the only method for investigating the process of the translation of the genetic code which is what I wanted to study.

The discovery was the real reason for my overwhelming feeling. The day we found an answer, we were all having a "Eureka!" moment. It was an incredible feeling, to finally get an answer after so much research. The Nobel Prize is great, but not as overwhelming as the actual finding.

Maya: *How do you think serving in the army helped shape your career?*

Ada: I served in the medical corps and learned a lot about biology.

Maya: *Were there any obstacles you faced while growing up? Did you have mentors who motivated you to pursue chemistry? Are there any role models you looked up to?*

Ada: For a long time (over 16 years), I was considered a dreamer or the village fool. We were poor, and my father died when I was 11, leaving behind my uneducated mom and my baby sister which was a huge challenge for our family. At that time, I started working multiple jobs such as babysitting, teaching, and others. I noticed that chemistry is required for understanding life processes which is something that I really wanted to look into which is why I studied that subject. I didn't have any role models, but I got inspiration from Marie Curie and Albert Einstein.

Maya: *How does it feel to be the first woman from the Middle East to have the highest honor by winning the Nobel Prize?*

Ada: The discovery was the real reason for my overwhelming feeling. The day we found an answer, we were all having a "Eureka!" moment. It was an incredible feeling, to finally get an answer after so much research. The Nobel Prize is great, but not as overwhelming as the actual finding. Additionally, being "first" or "only" has no meaning for me, it is the science and actual discovery that really matters to me.

Maya: *What are some of the other research areas in chemistry that are interesting to you?*

Ada: All-natural processes, including life processes are interesting for me.

Maya: *If you hadn't been a scientist, what career do you think you would have pursued?*

Ada: I wanted to be a writer.

Maya: *You have accomplished a lot. As a female leader in science, what advice do you have for young girls who want to be like you?*

Ada: My only advice is — "don't look for advice."

Maya: *If you could have lunch with someone alive or dead, who would it be?*

Ada: There are so many of such people, I could never choose between them.

Adena Friedman

President and CEO, Nasdaq

Adena Friedman is an American businesswoman who currently serves as the president and CEO of Nasdaq, the world's second-largest stock exchange in the world. As CEO of Nasdaq, Friedman is the first woman to lead a global exchange company. Before joining Nasdaq, she worked at The Carlyle Group as the CFO and Managing Director.

Maya: *What did you want to be as a child?*
Adena: Growing up, I wanted to be an astronaut. I had a fantastic science teacher who encouraged me to explore what it would take to be an astronaut — from a space camp to learning physics. There was never a point where someone discouraged me from my dreams or made me think it would be too hard. Instead, they were making sure I was prepared to succeed in whatever career I chose.

Maya: *As the CEO of Nasdaq, what does your job entail?*
Adena: My responsibilities as CEO of Nasdaq range from setting the strategic direction of the firm, shaping and driving

an inclusive culture, building consensus and making critical decisions, and ultimately making sure that we are performing for our clients and shareholders. As CEO of a global company, I need to have the breadth and depth to see and do many things, and I enjoy those challenges. I also need to trust the team around me and have faith in their decisions.

Maya: *What interested you in the world of finance and Wall Street?*

Adena: My father worked at an investment firm, and from a young age I always loved visiting his office and being on the trading floor. Though I didn't understand the ins and outs of the markets at the time, I was always intrigued by finance. Once I got a bit older and in graduate school, I was attracted to product management but was less interested in managing consumer goods. After speaking with my father, he pointed me in the direction of Nasdaq, where I could have the opportunity to manage technology products in the financial world. At the time Nasdaq was fairly unique in Financial Services. It was born as a financial technology company, so it uses technology as the foundation for everything it does. That made me very excited to work here when I was young and continues to be such an exciting element of my role today.

Maya: *You are the first women to be CEO of Nasdaq, how does that feel? What message does it send to young girls?*

Adena: Being named CEO was an incredibly proud moment for me, I was so grateful for the opportunity to lead this incredible company. I hope that it encourages young girls and women to be confident in their dreams and to set a bold career path. I didn't always dream of becoming a CEO, but as my

It is really important for girls to speak up — whether that is in school, at home, or in their careers. Finding one's voice early on will only help in the future. It is really up to you to work hard and to set your own ambitions. Nothing is handed to anyone, and you need to make the most of every situation.

career progressed, my ambition grew, and I realized that the skills I was developing would prepare me well for the CEO role. It is always important to have a goal to work toward, and to think through the steps to take to make it achievable.

Maya: *What can girls do in schools when they are young that will help them be ready for whatever is thrown at them?*
Adena: It is really important for girls to speak up — whether that is in school, at home, or in their careers. Finding one's voice early on will only help in the future. It is really up to you to work hard and to set your own ambitions. Nothing is handed to anyone, and you need to make the most of every situation.

Maya: *Do you or have you ever faced sexism throughout your career? And if so, how have you handled it?*
Adena: I am fortunate to have always worked at a company that values good work over anything else. I had great sponsors and mentors who were flexible when I needed — specifically when my children were young, and still encouraged me to take on a bigger role at work and give me more responsibility.

Maya: *How can we help society learn that women are as equally capable of anything as men are and should never be looked down upon?*
Adena: We are doing a good job in bringing this discussion to the forefront. I think that so far, no one is perfect, but it is a matter of making the work environment and hiring process more equal for all people. Whether that means mandating that diverse candidates are interviewed for every open position or making sure business leaders are held accountable for having a diverse workforce.

Maya: *You work in a fast-paced industry, how do you go about managing your time and workload with family life?*

Adena: Given that our business is a global one, we truly are on 24/7. With that being said, I learned early on that it is important to take the time to be with my family, whether that meant leaving a little early to go to one of my sons' sports games or working part-time for a few years when my children were born. It is certainly doable to have both a full work life and a full family life, but it's important to be communicative both with your peers and family. My husband and I are true partners in managing our family while also managing our careers. I also understand the importance of taking time for myself. I exercise regularly and that's an important part of my daily routine.

Maya: *How did going to an all-girls high school shape your viewpoints and you as a person?*

Adena: Going to an all-girls high school absolutely helped shape me as a person — I always felt that it was ok to be smart and to ask questions. I really loved math and science and was able to focus on succeeding in those areas without worrying about any of the pressures that sometimes come with a co-ed environment.

Maya: *What leadership principles do you live by?*

Adena: I am encouraged by Jeff Bezos' quote: "Every day is day one." At Nasdaq, and any tech company, there is no time for complacency — every day, I am always excited about what is to come and how we can continue to make the capital markets a more efficient and fairer place that facilitates capital formation, economic prosperity and job growth. That is something that I think you can feel at Nasdaq — we are a mission driven organization and all of us look forward to getting into work every day.

Maya: *Do you trust data or intuition in making big decisions?*
Adena: I think the best way to make big decisions is to use both.

Maya: *You have a black belt in Tae Kwon Do. What has it taught you and has it influenced you in how you work?*
Adena: Tae Kwon Do has taught me many things — it has impressed upon me the idea that everything is in my own control. If I want to get better, I need to make the decision to work hard. Nobody else is going to do that for me. It also helped take away the fear of getting punched — I know that I can get hit and it's not the worst thing in the world. I just need to decide to get back up afterwards.

Maya: *Technology is evolving at a fast pace, there are concerns about automation and jobs. What's your view of how the industries will be shaped by AI, 5G, robotics, and others?*
Adena: At Nasdaq, we see four aspects of technology that will reshape the markets and financial services of the future — cloud computing, machine intelligence, blockchain and quantum computing. These technologies will all change the way people make investment decisions and how they have access to the capital markets. But we also are looking at many other new emerging technologies. I'm excited about the things we are doing, and the energy level among our teams working with our clients is immensely gratifying. Being able to work on cutting edge and bleeding edge technologies is something that motivates me.

Dr. Ana Mari Cauce

President, University of Washington

Dr. Ana Mari Cauce is the first female president of the University of Washington. Cauce was raised in Miami, Florida after fleeing her home country during the Cuban Revolution. She earned her PhD at Yale University in psychology. Prior to her work at UW, Cauce was a lecturer at the University of Delaware. Cauce is a professor of Psychology and American Ethnic Studies, with secondary appointments in the Department of Gender, Women and Sexuality Studies and the College of Education. She maintains an active research program, focusing on adolescent development, with a special emphasis on at-risk youth. She is also a strong advocate for women and underrepresented minorities to pursue careers in science, technology, engineering and mathematics.

Maya: *As a leader of one of the biggest public universities in the world, what are some of the key leadership principles that you live by?*
Ana: While I don't think there are universal leadership principles that everyone can or should live by, I can share what

has worked for me, based on my own experiences. Over the years, I have learned the importance of bringing together a top team. You can't do it all yourself, no matter how good of a leader you are, so you need a team you can rely on. I simply could not lead this extraordinary university without a team to match it. The passion and talent of those at the University of Washington inspires me every day. To be an effective leader, it is important that I stay connected with this special community, which includes our students, faculty and staff, but also extends to our many alumni, donors and supporters around Washington and the world. They keep me focused on what matters most and the work ahead.

Maya: *How did you decide to be in the education field? What's the role of the university in shaping the human mind?*
Ana: My father started his career as a rural schoolteacher and worked his way up to being Minister of Education in Cuba. Although he and my mom were forced to take factory jobs to support their children, they never wavered in their belief that education was the key to a better life here in America. Their commitment to education has fueled me through my own life, first as a student and now in my career in higher education. I first became an educator because I wanted to make a difference, in the world and in students' lives. Like my parents, I strongly believe that education is critical to a healthier, more prosperous and more just and equitable society. Education, from pre-school to college and beyond, not only transforms individual lives, but the lives of entire communities and beyond, because those students go on to achieve great things that will help others thrive.

Maya: *What did you want to be when you were a child?*

Ana: As a young person who grew up in the Watergate era, I saw what powerful impact journalists, like Woodward and Bernstein, could have in protecting our democratic ideals. That inspired me to consider pursuing journalism as a career. In college, I discovered how much I loved research and my path shifted to child clinical psychology as a way to further that interest while also helping people.

Maya: *Did you have a mentor(s) in your early career days? How did they shape your thinking and your pursuit for greater good? Who have been your role models?*

Ana: As a graduate student at Yale, I had the privilege to be mentored by Edmund W. Gordon who, in turn, had been mentored by the legendary sociologist and activist W.E.B. Du Bois. These two individuals were great change-makers and I believe it is my responsibility to honor their legacy by doing the same. For me, the best way I can do that is to ensure students have access to excellent education and the boundless opportunities that come with the college experience.

Maya: *You have such an inspiring life-story. How does it feel to be named a "Great Immigrant"? What does that mean to you?*

Ana: It is truly an honor to be counted among such fabulous individuals. It is humbling to be part of a diverse group of leaders, artists, entrepreneurs, scholars and public servants who share the belief that our country is made stronger through our long tradition of welcoming immigrants.

Emerging technologies, including artificial intelligence, will be key to many careers in the years to come. So, we encourage all of our students, regardless of their chosen major, to become familiar with advances in computing and other technologies, because they will very likely be using those technologies in their careers after they graduate.

Maya: *Being a gay Cuban-American immigrant, were there any obstacles you had to face to get to the position you are in now? What helped you overcome them?*

Ana: I've been a witness to a whole host of changes in the United States over the course of my life, and one of the most important has been how we are becoming a more open and inclusive society — though we still have a long way to go. What helped me overcome the obstacles that I've faced, and that are faced by countless others across our country simply because of who they are, is being part of a supportive community and having mentors who were themselves trailblazers. You never know what someone else is facing, and so just the simple act of being kind and supportive to those around you is a wonderful way to help break down obstacles for others.

Maya: *AI (Artificial Intelligence) and automation are in the news every day. How is UW preparing the next generation of engineers and scholars for the AI era?*

Ana: Emerging technologies, including artificial intelligence, will be key to many careers in the years to come. So, we encourage all of our students, regardless of their chosen major, to become familiar with advances in computing and other technologies, because they will very likely be using those technologies in their careers after they graduate. For those planning to make a career in technology, we have a range of programs across the university, from computer science and engineering to human centered design, that will help them prepare for careers in a rapidly changing field.

Maya: *In an article about your population health initiative, you noted that you wanted to prepare for the effects of climate change. How can we spread awareness about climate change in a way that leads to meaningful change?*

Ana: Climate change is a serious threat to the health of communities and individuals, here and around the world. And so, it is incumbent upon universities, businesses and policymakers who recognize this threat to help share the clear scientific evidence of humans' role in creating climate change. Sharing information so that people can make informed decisions is a vital part of our mission as a public university dedicated to serving the people of Washington.

Maya: *The US is ranked poorly in STEM. What you think we need to do to get students, especially girls, interested in STEM early on? How do we create equality in jobs and get more women involved in leadership roles?*

Ana: Diversity and equity are core values of the University of Washington — they are essential to realizing our public mission to serve the greater good, and to the success of any business or organization. UW has been a leader in programs to support women in STEM, including our Women in Science and Engineering (WiSE) Program, which helps women succeed through mentorship and professional development opportunities. Programs like WiSE have proven successful to encourage more women to go into the STEM fields and women now make up 42 percent of undergraduate STEM majors, nearly double the figure from ten years ago. Despite this progress, we also recognize that sexism and inequalities in many forms continue to persist throughout our nation. These are challenging issues that we must confront and there is no better place to do that then at our nation's universities, and in partnership with leaders in business and society.

Maya: *What's the role of liberal arts in the life of an engineer and vice versa? What key characteristics have you seen in students who go on to become leaders in our society?*

Ana: It is important to the University of Washington, and to me personally, that we provide all of our students with a well-rounded liberal arts education. The complex challenges we face, whether as individuals or as a society, require us to understand and appreciate different viewpoints. It is not enough that an engineer can design a new bridge, they also have to effectively communicate their plans to construction managers in order for it to be physically built. By the same token, an art student not only needs to know theories of art but also how design software works. A broad-based education is also essential for our democracy, which depends on an informed and engaged citizenry.

Maya: *What do you like to do when you have some free time?*

Ana: I really enjoy those moments I get to spend time at home with my wife Susan and our dog Sally, and our newest additions to the family, our cats Stillwater and Annie. I also love to go hiking and be surrounded by the stunning beauty that we have all over Washington.

Maya: *What advice would you give to your younger self?*

Ana: I'd probably tell myself to be a bit more patient, that things will happen in their due course. Planning is important and it's good to have a sense of direction and goals. But it's also important to take some time to enjoy the moment and take advantage of opportunities that call out to you, even if they end up being a side-trip away from the main pathway you're on.

Ann Crady Weiss

Entrepreneur and Venture Capitalist, True Ventures

Ann Crady Weiss is the founder and current CEO of Hatch (previously Hatch Baby), a company which supports new parents, as well as a True Ventures partner. Weiss was introduced to the entrepreneurship industry at a young age as she would often go door-to-door or set up lemonade stands. She started her career working as a corporate securities attorney and then working for Yahoo! as a business development director. She later founded two companies called Maya's Mom (bought by Johnson & Johnson) and Hatch. Weiss enjoys helping entrepreneurs in their early stages as well as beginning consumer internet, mobile, and IoT companies.

Maya: *How did you come up with the idea of Hatch Baby?*
Ann: I was inspired to start Hatch Baby for two reasons. The first reason is because I am a mom with three kids, and I've known what it's like to become a new parent three times, so, I have a personal connection with Hatch Baby. The second reason is because there is a significant business opportunity. When you look at the market that we play in, which is markets

I believe that the most important characteristic of a founder is grit. You know you have to be willing and committed to getting the job done, no matter what, you are not going to quit.

for products and services for new families, they spend $12,000 a year on their babies and their young children which is a lot of money. So, it's a significant business opportunity that I was uniquely positioned to go after not only because I am a mom, but because I have spent my career working on mobile and engagement related to new moms and dads.

Maya: *On your website, I noticed that your startup was related to Internet of Things. What are your thoughts on data privacy with respect to Internet of Things?*

Ann: I think privacy is super important. We've seen examples where things have gone wrong and it's devastating for the brand but also for the human beings that are affected. It's a really big deal to have their data stolen or compromised which is why we take it very seriously. Everything we design is designed with the user in mind. Earning and keeping that user trust is extremely important so security is a huge deal for us.

Maya: *You have started a couple of companies so what do you think are some of the leadership principles that you live by in good times and bad times?*

Ann: In general, I believe that the most important characteristic of a founder is grit. You know you have to be willing and committed to getting the job done, no matter what, you are not going to quit. I also think it's important to be really smart and to be someone who has a passion and can share their passion to get other people excited about their own passion. You can't create a company by yourself, and so your belief has to be infectious. It's grit, intelligence and having the ability to inspire and communicate your mission or your belief. The other thing that is extremely important, is emotional intelligence. You have to be able to forgive yourself for making mistakes and celebrate yourself or successes and do the same thing for your team. It is so important to have a good sense of self-awareness, and know things you're strong at, and also not as strong, so you can build a team of confidence.

Maya: *Was there ever a time where you had a really hard time while starting your company?*
Ann: Totally! Starting and running is the best job I've ever had personally. But it's also the worst job I've ever had because it is so incredibly hard and anyone that has been or is a founder or CEO of a company who says to you, "Oh starting a company isn't that hard!" is either a liar, or they have only been trying for a couple of days. The struggle to keep going when there's a major bug in your hardware or when you have a really key employee quit is important. There are so many examples of things that can go wrong that are devastating and again this is why you have to go back to the most important characteristic: grit. You just got to keep on going.

Maya: *As an investor, what do you look for in an entrepreneur and their ideas?*
Ann: There are three things that we look for at True Ventures. By far the most important factor in being successful is the founding team. It is the team that is going to make themselves successful because if you don't have a group or a protagonist who has the characteristics that I was talking about earlier, then, it doesn't matter how great your idea is, it's not going to go anywhere. The second thing I look for is a market that has unconstrained upsides. What I mean by that is, we are not interested in investing in someone who wants to replace all of

the windows in the world because the reality is, we know what the window market is and there isn't really a ton of differentiation that would make everyone in the world want to take out their windows and use our new windows. We know how big that market is. We want to invest in companies with unconstrained upside where if their crazy idea works, it has potential to either create a new market, or transform and grow an existing market. That's the kind of idea that we're looking for and the way we describe that at True Ventures is called the blue ocean market. The third thing we look for is the stage of the deal. For example, we have a fund that is set up to do early stage investment and basically what that means is we want to be the first professional money that an entrepreneur takes. The deal has to be our kind of deal, like an early stage deal, we don't start new companies when they have 50 people. We like to start the company when they have one or two people in it.

Maya: *How do you find a balance between work and family time?*

Ann: When I leave my office and I have time with my kids and my husband, I try to put my phone down and not take meeting because the time with my family is just with my family. And then when my kids go to sleep, I work again sometimes. For me and I hope for everyone that works at Hatch Baby, family comes first. If you have a dance recital or a field trip to go to with your child, it's really important to prioritize that. Going back to one of the things that I was talking about the qualities of a founder, I want to fund and be a person who is a well-rounded, happy and healthy individual because if you're happy and healthy, only then will you be effective in your job.

Maya: *What do you think is the key traits in a person for them to be able to become an entrepreneur?*

Ann: It takes grit and it takes motivation to create something substantial and lasting. It also takes intelligence and you need to have the ability to communicate with others.

Arianna Huffington

Founder of Huffington Post and Founder and CEO of Thrive Global

Arianna Huffington is a Greek-American businesswoman and a well-established author. She is the founder of The Huffington Post, a news and blog website, and the founder and current CEO of Thrive Global, a company whose mission is to enhance the well-being and performance of their consumers. Huffington has been in Time Magazine's list of The World's 100 Most Influential People as well as Forbes's Most Powerful Women list. She earned her B.A. in economics at the famed Cambridge University. Huffington served on many boards such as Uber, Onex, and Global Citizen.

Maya: *Who has been the biggest influence in your life? How have they shaped you into who you are?*
Arianna: The biggest influence in my life has always been my mother. She had the gift of living in a constant state of wonder at the world around her. Whether she was washing dishes, feeding seagulls at the beach, or reprimanding overworking businessmen, she maintained her sense of wonder at life.

Whenever I'd complain or was upset about something in my own life, my mother would always give me the piece of advice, "Darling, just change the channel. You are in control of the clicker. Don't replay the bad, scary movie." Her other favorite piece of advice to me was that failure isn't the opposite of success, but a stepping stone. That gave my sister and me the encouragement and license to try anything and secure with the knowledge that if we failed, she wouldn't love us any less.

Maya: *Lately, you have become such a big advocate for sleep and meditation. How did you come about to the realization that these are critical elements to maintain our sanity?*

Arianna: My mother actually taught my younger sister Agapi and I how to meditate when I was thirteen years old. Growing up, meditation was seen as a cure for just about everything. In fact, my mother had convinced us that if we meditated, we would be able to do our homework faster and improve our grades. We knew that meditation made us more peaceful and less upset when things didn't go our way, but we also realized that it made us happier. Now, science has provided evidence to back this all up. If anything, my mother was underselling the benefits of meditation. Science has caught up to ancient wisdom, and the results are overwhelming and unambiguous. As for sleep, I had a wake-up call in 2007 when I collapsed from exhaustion and lack of sleep. I'd just returned home from a college tour with my daughter, Christina, who was a junior in high school at the time. The ground rules we'd agreed on — or, more accurately, that Christina demanded — were that during the days I would not be on my phone. So, every night after dinner, I stayed up late working after Christina went to sleep.

The morning after we got back, I collapsed from exhaustion, hitting my head on my way down, cutting my eye and breaking my cheekbone. Afterwards, as I went to various doctors to find out what the underlying medical problem was, I had a chance to ask myself a lot of questions about the kind of life I was living. Was this the life I wanted? Is this really what success looks like? After the diagnosis came in, an acute case of burnout, I gradually began to make changes in my life. These changes included renewing my estranged relationship with sleep. And in fact, as I learned more about sleep — the history of it, the science, and the increasing number of studies that show how deeply connected sleep is to our well-being, performance and productivity — I became a sleep evangelist. And that led me to write *Thrive and The Sleep Revolution* and, ultimately, founding Thrive Global.

Maya: *What is success in your mind? Is it working nearly 24/7 or is it making your well-being your first priority and work second? How soon do you think people (students) should start considering a balanced life?*
Arianna: I would define success as living a life filled with well-being, wisdom, wonder and the power of giving. My mother certainly met that definition of success — she was all about living in the moment, connecting deeply with everybody who crossed her path (often over food), and giving anything and everything she had (her time, her possessions, etc.) that she thought might give joy to someone else. And it's not really about balance. Work and life, well-being and productivity, are not on opposite sides — so they don't need to be balanced. They're on the same side and rise in tandem. Increase one and

Workplaces fueled by strong masculine pride and burnout, makes it hard for women to advance. This is part of what I think of as the Third Women's Revolution. It's about going beyond access and getting our foot in the door and toward changing workplace cultures that undervalue women in ways that are both subtle and not subtle.

you increase the other, which is what the science clearly shows. So, it's never too early to start prioritizing your well-being because you'll increase your productivity and performance in school, and you'll be laying the foundation for habits that will give you a huge competitive advantage long-term!

Maya: *The technology industry has struggled to provide equal opportunities to women. In your mind, what are the main reasons for this and how do we get more women in leadership positions more quickly?*

Arianna: Gender parity and inclusiveness are obviously incredibly important and have been priorities throughout my entire career. But it's not just about hiring, as vital as that is. It's also about changing the day-to-day culture. Workplaces fueled by strong masculine pride and burnout, makes it hard for women to advance. This is part of what I think of as the Third Women's Revolution. It's about going beyond access and getting our foot in the door and toward changing workplace cultures that undervalue women in ways that are both subtle and not subtle. Women must be in workplaces that work for them. And they also have the most incentive to change it, because they pay when burnout and long hours are taken as a proxy for commitment and dedication. Even when they are working, women are doing the lion's share of the work of keeping up the household, which is a backdoor way of excluding women or at least making it harder for them to advance. That's one more reason for why it's so important to change this culture of burnout — which, by the way, will also benefit men. Women can do this by helping other women and bringing them in. At the Uber all-hands meeting I was at, as I was introducing Uber's second female board member, Wan Ling Martello from Nestle, I pointed out that one of the biggest variables in adding a woman to a leadership position is that somewhere there is another woman already in a leadership position there.

Maya: *How do you think paying more attention to your well-being has helped you succeed?*
Arianna: What I've learned since prioritizing well-being in my life, is that I'm not only more productive, calmer, less stressed, more creative and make better decisions, but now I feel more present to enjoy my life and be present for those around me. When we prioritize our well-being, our performance goes up across every metric, including in school. For instance, not getting enough sleep compromises decision-making and recall, so it's better to get enough sleep the night before a test than it is to stay up all night studying!

Maya: *What is one of your most favorite quotes to go by or read every day for motivation?*
Arianna: "Live life as if everything is rigged in your favor" — Rumi.

Maya: *You have traveled around the globe. Which is your favorite city to visit and why?*
Arianna: I always love visiting India, and we launched Thrive Global there earlier this year. I first went when I was 17 to study comparative religion at Viva-Bharati University, outside of Calcutta. And in between studies, I traveled across the country, falling in love with it. It's a love affair that has continued to this day, so I'll always go back.

Maya: *If you could have lunch with any person dead or alive, who would it be and why?*

Arianna: It would be Marcus Aurelius because his stoic approach to life, where we can't control what happens in the external world, but we can control how we respond, has never been more relevant.

Maya: *What advice would you give to your younger self?*

Arianna: I'd tell my younger self to not buy into the delusion that the necessary price to become successful is burnout and exhaustion.

Ashley Parker

Pulitzer Prize Winning Journalist at Washington Post

Ashley Parker is one of the world's foremost journalist, a familiar face on television, and a strong voice of reason amidst the crazy political environment of our nation. Parker is a veteran journalist who was awarded the highest honor in journalism — the Pulitzer Prize for her fearless and in-depth reporting. She spent 11 years at New York Times before joining Washington Post in 2017. She did her BA in English and Communications from University of Pennsylvania.

Maya: *You have been a journalist for quite a while now, how do you think journalism has helped you learn more about yourself and the world around you?*

Ashley: In a number of ways. My first job in journalism was a research assistant for Maureen Dowd — who is a New York Times columnist, where I got to do a little bit of everything. And so that experience alone, I felt like left me with not just a lot of really good journalism skills, but also great ways of approaching different things. In addition to her being a great mentor, I learned the skills of perseverance, diligence and hard work. Speaking more generally, one of the best parts of being a journalist, especially as a political reporter first of all, it almost never feels like work, and when you're older, you'll realize you are incredibly lucky to have a job that doesn't feel like you need to be going to the desk all night. As I covered different campaigns, I've traveled the country. I've been able to travel to cover everything from a really fancy fundraiser in California to getting to know wealthy donors to spending a lot of time in small towns across the country that were ravaged by the opioid crisis or the financial crises. I have been able to go out and talk to people, not just the political operatives, and the ad makers and donors but was able to talk to actual voters, small business owners and people whose livelihoods were actually affected by the policies in Washington DC. All this has changed how I understand the world and especially the U.S.

Maya: *You graduated from Penn with a major in creative writing. Did you know that you wanted to do journalism right after graduating college? Or did it take you a while to figure that out? What inspired you to be a journalist?*
Ashley: I knew right away that the only thing I wanted to do was to be a journalist. I probably knew this in high school. In college, I had worked for the college newspaper and journalism internships. I majored in creative writing, which was a lot of writing workshops and so I was almost 100% sure that the only thing I wanted to be was a journalist. I should have some good answers as to why I wanted to be a journalist like, the pursuit of truth or holding institutions accountable, etc. But the truth is that since I was a little kid, I have always loved writing and telling stories. To me, journalism feels like

the poor man's version of writing. If I had any good plots, I bet I would be just as happy being a novelist or, having grown up in LA, I might be just as happy being a television writer. As a journalist, you get to go out and learn about different people's stories every single day and then tell those stories through your own writing and that's just something I've always loved.

Maya: *I've read some of your articles in the Washington Post and was wondering how you're able to write so eloquently and in just a short amount of time.*

Ashley: It never feels super eloquent. It always feels like panic and frantic and up against deadline. You can ask any journalist and they would say the same thing that writing on a deadline is a very compelling force. So, in a way, having a crushing deadline where you know you have to file your story, and you know your editor has to have it because if they don't, there will be a hole in the paper the next day, really focuses the mind and makes time pass pretty quickly. One thing about the Washington Post that's great, is that it's very much a writer's paper, which means that you don't get assignments from your editors. I work very closely with my editors on all of my stories, sort of talking through everything from the idea to the recording, to how should I go about the lead, and how long should it be, what's the right tone. They really do let you be a little more creative, and experimental and push the envelope. I cover the White House, which is pretty serious but there's a lot of fun scenes and unusual things that unfold. At the Washington Post, they encourage you to go and be an observer and write what you see in a fun creative way.

Maya: *How do you balance your own bias with reporting facts while you're writing?*

Ashley: I would argue that I don't have a tremendous ideological bias. If you really were someone who was super moved on a particular issue, there are enough publications, both conservative and liberal, where you can write with a point of view. I think journalists are inherently observers by nature and not activists. That being said, I'm sure I have the biases from just my own upbringing and where I grew up, where I went to school, and who I am friends with. I think, at the end of the day, the way to get the best stories — which is what journalists want — is to just tell the facts in front of you, in a fair and as accurate way as possible. In this White House, where you often have different people with different agendas and different versions of the truth, one has to be especially diligent. For me, that means talking to as many people as possible and not just writing a story based on something that one or two people told me and to my colleagues but talking to dozens of people, it is sort of talking to all of those people to create a kind of a kaleidoscope to get a 360 degrees sense of what has actually happened. I think just by focusing on what the facts are, what you are hearing and the people you are talking for a story is a good and easy way to keep your biases, even subconscious ones, out.

Maya: *How do you develop and maintain good sources for your pieces?*

Ashley: In general, I think it's always better, especially as you're getting to know people, to try to meet them in person. I would rather meet someone in person, even if they don't want to talk to me on record or even if they don't want to talk to me about a story. I will always make a pitch to meet someone in person, just so they know who I am. At the very least, they know what I look like if they want to call me up and yell at me for something I did or said or wrote about. Another thing I try to do is to be as upfront as possible. Not all my sources are going to like what I write. Sometimes they do, sometimes they don't, and sometimes they don't care. But I can't control the story or facts on the ground for example, if the White House had a bad day, I'm going to write that. If President Trump did something historic, then I'll write that. What I can control is being honest and upfront with my sources. If I'm talking to someone about a story or writing something about them, I try to give everyone a heads up and as full of awareness as possible, of what the story is going to say, what the angle of the story will be. If I'm writing something, really tough on Jared Kushner tied to the White House, then before the story gets published, Jared and everyone on his team will have a good sense of what's going to be in the story.

Maya: *While writing your columns, do you ever think about how the public might react to your writing?*
Ashley: I try not to because, first of all, I think it's distracting and unhelpful; secondly, I'm actually a really bad judge of that. There will be stories I've written that will go viral, and people will really like them. And there are other stories that I write, I feel like no one reads them or clicks on them. Then there are also stories that I just bang out on my iPhone while I am walking between the White House and my office and people go crazy about them. There are profiles that I've written on people where I think the subject is going to be really happy and flattered and curious as to how I described the tone of their

voice. And there are other profiles where I think, this person is not going to like it, but that person is thrilled and flattered and wants me to send copies of the Washington Post to hang up on their wall. I also have a really poor barometer of how the public will feel about a certain piece.

Maya: *How do you think that increased use of social media has impacted journalism?*

Ashley: Journalists live on Twitter all day long. And they use it as a place to see what your competitors are writing, as a place to see what the president is thinking and saying, and as a place to promote your own stories. Sometimes I think that is really bad for our brains to be that connected. It's hard to sit down and do four hours of really good writing, if you're checking Twitter every five minutes. But I feel like I end up doing my best thinking when I'm either in the shower, out for a run, or on the back of my husband's Vespa. And those are the three places where I can't check my phone. So, journalists definitely do pay attention to social media. I think it's an important part of how we do our job, especially with our current president. But I think it may also be having a corrosive effect. One thing that's interesting is the president tweets and what he tweets ends up getting to the general public very quickly, but it's not necessarily because they all have Twitter, or they're all following the president on Twitter. It's actually the tweets end up on cable news or articles that we write. At the end of the day, it does create an ecosystem system and echo chamber where this president in particular, is able to get a message out to his voters through social media almost instantaneously, even if the way they consume isn't social media — it may be TV, radio, the nightly news, or newspapers.

Maya: *How does it feel to be awarded one of journalism's top prizes?*

Ashley: I just feel incredibly lucky. I won it for being part of a much larger team of people. So, I just feel so lucky that I started at the Washington Post right when Trump became president. I was thrown into big, incredible, and amazing stories. I got to work with best colleagues in the business who are not just amazing writers and reporters, but they're also a ton of fun. I never imagined that I would win a Pulitzer. I never aspired to win a Pulitzer. But, if I was going to win one, it feels very fitting that I would do it with a team effort with everyone else at the paper.

Maya: *How do you think that leadership traits play out in your job as a journalist?*

Ashley: We have a lot of good leaders around the newsroom. I mean, in a way, you have writers and editors, but journalism often kind of feels fairly flat and there is less of a hierarchy than you would have in a law firm or a hedge fund where there is one president or a CEO and then everyone else below. So, it feels very collaborative to be a journalist and I definitely rely on my editors to help me think of ideas and help save me from myself. But for a lot of reporters, you're likely to get a great idea from a brainstorm with a colleague or asking a colleague to help you confirm a detail or just think through a way of telling a story. For example, I'm in politics, but being able to walk across the newsroom to someone who covers economics and financial issues all day to help you read a financial disclosure form is incredibly useful. I guess that's the long way of saying there are different leaders all over the newsroom who you can rely on for different things.

You also have to be good at handling rejection when you call someone and they hang up on you, or you show up at someone's door and they don't open it, or they open it and then just slam it in your face. So, be good at handling rejections, or if you're not good at handling rejection then get good. Be hard working and persistent.

Maya: *What was your favorite article to write for The Washington Post and why?*

Ashley: One specific article that I wrote even before it was one of the stories that were in the package that won a Pulitzer, was a story I did with a couple of colleagues where we broke the news, that President Trump has dictated the misleading statement to his son Donald Trump Jr. about a meeting that his son had with a Russian lawyer in Trump Tower during the campaign. I just liked it because it felt so different from what I normally do. It felt like the investigative work and a story that took us a while and it was hard to get. It was getting one little piece of the puzzle and putting our heads together and then going back and figuring out the next piece. And that was not a type of journalism I do all the time. It was out of my comfort zone and I was proud of that story. In general, my favorite collection of articles is this thing we have at the Washington Post called a debrief, and it's similar to explaining something about the president or the White House or the Easter Egg Roll on the South Lawn, that is really small. I do a lot of debriefs at different moments of his presidency and those are, in general, probably some of my favorite stories to do because you get to write in a fun, whimsical way.

Maya: *What advice do you have for young journalists?*

Ashley: I would say that if you actually want to be a journalist, which you should, it's a ton of fun. I think it is the most fun you can have in a job as an adult. However, as a young journalist, you should be able to handle rejections because it can be a tough field to break into. You also have to be good at handling rejection when you call someone and they hang up on you, or you show up at someone's door and they don't open it, or they open it and then just slam it in your face. So, be good at handling rejections, or if you're not good at handling rejection then get good. Be hard working and persistent. Also, coming early to work or do the assignments that no one else wants to do because it involves driving for three hours will help you get some amazing stories.

Beth Comstock

Former Vice Chair, General Electric

Beth Comstock is the former vice chair of General Electric (GE), a company that works with healthcare, power, renewable energy, aviation, digital industry, and many more. GE is considered one of the most pioneering companies that has lasted over 150 years. Comstock became the first female to occupy the office of vice chair at GE. Comstock started her career in local television in Virginia. Before serving as GE's chief marketing and commercial officer, Comstock worked as President of Integrated Media at NBC Universal, and also served at NBC, CBS, and Turner Broadcasting. She was on Forbes list of The World's 100 Most Powerful Women in both 2015 and 2016.

Maya: *What did you want to be when you were growing up?*
Beth: I found a note recently that I wrote when I was 14 which said I wanted to be 50 different things when I grow up, including a mountain climber! When I went to college, I thought I wanted to be a doctor and then a journalist.

Maya: *You became the first female to hold the title of Vice Chair at GE. You have also been called one of the most powerful women in business. How does that feel? And what message does it send to young girls?*

Beth: It's nice when you get recognized but, at the same time, it's just the opinion of a few people. And the next year, you're just as likely to be off the list. I always liked the recognition especially for my colleagues and company. So, my advice is to enjoy the recognition, but don't let it define you.

Maya: *How can we get the world to pay more attention to STEM, especially girl's STEM education? How can we get more girls involved in technology at an early stage?*

Beth: I think girls need to be exposed to STEM in more creative ways, to see the impact of technology — for example, how it's saving lives in healthcare or reducing emissions in the climate. Additionally, how it is embedded in things they do every day, such as the internet, and they especially have to see women who have jobs in STEM — people like Mae Jemison who was an astronaut. When my younger daughter was in middle school, she was invited to be in the math and science club, but she turned it down saying she didn't see any girls in there. What a missed opportunity!

Maya: *There seems to be a big shift in technology with AI, blockchain, robotics, IoT, and other new technologies coming together. What changes do you anticipate in our society as a result? How will automation impact jobs? Will robots be a net positive or negative to the society?*

Beth: I worry about people turning into robots long before they will have to work for one. What I mean by this is that in the machine age, as more automation happens, we humans will

The best advice I've gotten is to ask for help from others. I got that feedback from some of my colleagues earlier in my career because they felt that I was only developing ideas but not asking for input. I also had to take my own advice to open up, meaning work hard to get over my reserved nature and connect more with other people.

be called on to be more creative and strategic. Yet many of our jobs are developed on repeatable process or focus only on the data, not challenging us to creatively solve new problems in new ways. If people just wait to be told what to do, they are acting like a robot. People need to use their imaginations to think up new solutions and ideas.

Maya: *What leadership principles do you live by?*
Beth: Make room for discovery, open up to what's next and new. And assume the best in others.

Maya: *You were given a job offer from Steve Jobs twice, and both times you turned it down. Why was that and what did you take away from that moment?*
Beth: They weren't the right jobs for me at the time. I sometimes regretted the decision, especially given Apple's success. But I also made the decision based on a strategic decision about what I wanted to do, what I was good at. I trusted my instinct.

Maya: *What's the best advice have you gotten and from whom?*
Beth: The best advice I've gotten is to ask for help from others. I got that feedback from some of my colleagues earlier in my career because they felt that I was only developing ideas but not asking for input. I also had to take my own advice to open up, meaning work hard to get over my reserved nature and connect more with other people. I'm very proud of overcoming my shyness and my introversion to push myself to meet and connect with others.

Maya: *Have you had mentors in the early part of your career?*
Beth: I've had some good mentors but more often than not, I've followed a "board of advisors" model where I seek advice from a range of people with different experiences.

Maya: *There is a huge gender pay gap and it seems like things keep deteriorating. Whose responsibility is it to fix the problem — industry, policy makers, others?*
Beth: The leaders of companies need to prioritize hiring, developing and paying well to women, people of color and in general people who are different. There are no excuses. It takes time and hard work, but it is possible.

Maya: *As someone who has worked with a lot of entrepreneurs, what are some of the traits that makes someone successful?*
Beth: Entrepreneurs are everywhere, not just in startups. To me an entrepreneur is someone who sees a better way and is driven to make it happen. We need entrepreneurs as nurses, teachers and in our government. What makes them successful is a passion for the mission of doing better and a resilience to keep trying in the face of a lot of adversity, which is what I call a "no is not yet" mindset.

Maya: *What inspired you to write the book 'Imagine It Forward'? What's the central message of the book?*
Beth: I was inspired to write the book as a way to chronicle the hard work, struggle and messiness that comes with change. Also, I wanted to offer people who are mid to early career some encouragement and practice tools for navigating change.

Maya: *You are a very busy executive, what are some of your hobbies and activities to recharge yourself?*
Beth: I love reading and writing. I love to travel; my favorite place is where I haven't been yet. I also enjoy spending time hiking in nature and enjoying art.

Maya: *What advice would you give to your younger self?*
Beth: Not to worry so much. If you work hard and mean well, you will do well. And your definition of success changes over time. To me, success about being part of a great team, doing our best work, and having an impact. I wouldn't have known that as a young woman starting out.

Dr. Ellen Ochoa

NASA Astronaut

Dr. Ellen Ochoa is a retired NASA astronaut who was Johnson Space Center's second female director. She was the first Hispanic woman to go into space on a nine-day STS-56 mission on the space shuttle Discovery back in 1993. Ochoa received her bachelor's degree in physics from San Diego State University as well as a master's degree and doctorate in electrical engineering from Stanford University. Ochoa worked as a research engineer at Sandia National Laboratories and at NASA Ames Research Center where she studied optical systems used for information processing. Ochoa has been recognized with NASA's highest award, the Distinguished Service Medal, and the Presidential Distinguished Rank Award.

Maya: *How do we inspire more girls to get into space or more generally, in STEM fields?*
Ellen: Many people and groups are working on this! Part of it is introducing girls to more hands-on activities and problem-solving teams so that they can see how they can use their

creativity and desire to improve the world through STEM fields.

Maya: *Did you ever doubt yourself if you should become an astronaut? If so, what did you tell yourself?*

Ellen: I really never expected to be selected as an astronaut because so many people apply, and only a few are chosen. I also didn't really have a background that seemed to fit with what other astronauts have. So, to get to my goal, I chose to take some actions that would help make me a better candidate: getting a private pilot's license (and thus learning about operational environments and making quick decisions), continuing to progress in my engineering research career, and moving to a job at a NASA research center.

Maya: *What is one thing about space that you find absolutely astounding?*

Ellen: How much it makes you appreciate Planet Earth.

Maya: *What does being the world's first Hispanic female astronaut mean to you?*

Ellen: It's given me a wonderful opportunity to reach out to people — including many Hispanic students — about the importance of education and the interesting and rewarding careers available in STEM.

Maya: *With the AI era coming up just around the corner, what does the future of astronomy and space travel look like?*

Ellen: The machine learning part of AI is certainly providing the ability to sift through massive amounts of data to make connections, learn new insights, and suggest new lines of

Set high goals for yourself and work towards them — whether or not you actually reach them, you will still be in a better place than if you hadn't tried. Opportunities only come to those who are prepared and have worked hard in whatever they have tried.

inquiry — which is exciting not only for astronomy but for all sciences. Also, the ability of spacecraft and robotic assistants to perform "dangerous, dirty, and dull" tasks will free up astronaut's time to spend on analytical tasks that are still very difficult for machines to do.

Maya: *What would you tell your younger self about aspiring to be an astronaut?*
Ellen: It's not as impossible as it seems! Set high goals for yourself and work towards them — whether or not you actually reach them, you will still be in a better place than if you hadn't tried. Opportunities only come to those who are prepared and have worked hard in whatever they have tried.

Emily Chang

Broadcast Journalist and News Anchor, Bloomberg

Emily Chang is an American journalist and a bestselling author. She is the executive producer of Bloomberg Technology which is a daily show focusing on global technology. She is also the producer of Bloomberg Studio 1.0, a show where she talks with top executives, investors, and entrepreneurs. Chang is the author of the national bestseller, *Brotopia: Breaking Up the Boys' Club of Silicon Valley* which dives into the sexism and gender inequalities in the tech industry. She graduated from Harvard University with a B.A. magna cum laude in Social Studies. Prior to her work in Bloomberg, she served as an international correspondent for CNN based in Beijing and London.

Maya: *You graduated from Harvard with a B.A. in social studies. What inspired you to go from a career in social studies to journalism?*
Emily: What's interesting is that I actually started my career at Harvard as a pre-med student as I thought I wanted to be a doctor. But after the first semester, I decided that I wanted to spend more time talking to my classmates, because they all

have such fascinating backgrounds, and one of the majors they were having had some really thoughtful and provocative conversations and that was social studies, which is basically a mix of political science, economics, psychology, sociology, history, philosophy, etc. So, I had the opportunity to explore a lot of different subjects and enjoy having conversations, I actually love asking questions and have a natural curiosity, which is always a good quality for a journalist. I like talking to people about their stories, and that's what I do every single day now. My job is really an everyday education, which is what motivates me to go to work every day.

Maya: *What is the main message that you want to send to someone who is reading your book, Brotopia?*
Emily: Women are, unfortunately, underrepresented in the tech industry. That goes for engineers and programmers as well as investors and entrepreneurs. It makes zero sense for half the population to not have a voice in an industry that is shaping the world. I mean, Silicon Valley is connecting the world, building self-driving cars, building rocket ships, and making products that are used by billions and billions of people and has a greater impact on our lives than any other industry out there. It's really important for people of all backgrounds to have a voice in this industry that have the potential to change the world.

Maya: *You started writing the book before the #MeToo movement. How did this new theme help to shape your book?*
Emily: I honestly had no idea when I started writing the book that we would be in the middle of this cultural movement. We are certainly having a moment and my hope is that we start to see real change as a result of the conversations we are having.

We're at risk of rewriting all of these wrongs for another 30 years. So, in my view, the tech industry has a responsibility right now to make a dramatic change, or women will be left out for the next 30 years.

When I was writing the book, many of the women I spoke to were a bit nervous about sharing their stories, because it's scary, and it's risky. But over the course of my reporting, and as the #MeToo movement unfolded, many of them decided to open up and they found their courage by finding collective courage. They saw others being brave and decided that, if not now, then, when would be a better time to try to make a difference.

Maya: *How do you think that society would have been different if women had been equal to men since the beginning of the tech revolution?*

Emily: Oh! In so many ways! I interviewed the co-founder of Twitter, Evan Williams, who told me he thinks online harassment and trolling wouldn't be such a problem if more women had been on the early Twitter team. So, imagine if the internet was a friendlier place, imagine if video games were less violent, imagine if we had better parental controls. Facial recognition technology, it doesn't recognize women and people of color as easily and accurately, as it does for white men. We're at risk of rewriting all of these wrongs for another 30 years. So, in my view, the tech industry has a responsibility right now to make a dramatic change, or women will be left out for the next 30 years.

Maya: *In your opinion, what is the hardest thing in journalism?*

Emily: I think all journalists have to find the courage to tell tough stories. We all have to be tough, but fair, and finding that balance is one of the hardest jobs of any journalist. In my line of work, I'm doing a live TV show every single day, and one of the most important things to do is to listen in order to do a good interview. It's not just about asking questions, it's about listening to the answers on the call, coming up with new questions that will lead to new insights. So being a good listener is something that I always strive to do to tell the most accurate, and enlightening, stories.

Maya: *How do you think that social media has helped shape journalism?*

Emily: The news comes out by the second on Twitter, and so the term breaking news means a whole different notion these days. In some respects, it can undermine the accuracy of news because a lot of the information that you get at first may not be the correct information or the correct analysis of the information. But on the other side, social media has given everyone a voice, which means that people and organizations are increasingly being held accountable. Although, it is a great thing, we certainly have to be careful of jumping to conclusions and making sure that we are reporting something that we have the sourcing to back it up, but I think the fact that platforms like Twitter and Facebook give everyone a voice, and a voice directly to the public is extremely important.

Maya: *Is it easy or hard to not have a bias when you are researching your story or interviewing someone?*

Emily: You know, I've been trained my entire career to be objective, and not share my personal opinion, so it's almost second nature to me. But, while writing the book, I came out with a much stronger point of view which, to be honest, was a little scary, but I felt like it was an important point of view and a worthy cause to provide support behind. So, whenever I'm doing a story or an interview, I work incredibly hard to be as fair and objective as possible, and also make sure that I'm trying to get to the truth.

Maya: *What is your favorite thing in journalism? Or what is the best part of getting to interview people such as Mark Zuckerberg and other CEOs?*

Emily: It's fascinating to have access to people who are on different lines of literally changing the world. I do think that the best part of the job is that I learn something new every single day. There's always something going on — it's never boring. There are always people with interesting things to say, and so, like I said, it's an everyday education and there's never a dull moment.

Maya: *How do you think leadership traits play out in your career?*

Emily: I think confidence is really important for any leader. As I have learned more about the subject that I'm covering, I've become more confident in my ability to tell these stories and the questions that I asked. I also think that being a good leader means being able to be part of the team. I have a team at work that I rely on every day, and I had an incredible team when I was writing my book as well. We are only as good as the teams that we are a part of, and I think it's really important for any leader to recognize that.

Maya: *Personally, for me, it's hard to maintain a schoolwork schedule as well as spend time with family. How do you find time to maintain your work as a journalist and also be a mom?*

Emily: My first job, and my most important job, is being a mom. But I also want my children to value my work and what I do because I love it. It's really important to convey that message to them that mommy's job is important, and she is trying to make a difference in the world. Writing a book wasn't easy, and it certainly took time away from my family, but I constantly tried to explain to them why I was doing it and why I thought it would make a difference. Personally, I'll say that I never feel like I have everything under control, and I have to juggle this perpetual state of imbalance. But I couldn't do the job I do without having the incredible family that I have, and I don't think I'd be as good of a mom if I didn't do the job that I do. I think both parts of my life make me a better person and, hopefully, my kids recognize that when they grow up.

Maya: *Reflecting back on your career, what are you most proud of?*
Emily: I'm proud of writing a book. I'm proud of building the show from scratch. Bloomberg technology was sort of like my own little startup. Most importantly, I'm proud of the way that I tell stories and do them justice. I work really hard to get to the heart of a story and get to the truth. My book is the product of over 300 interviews and even though I have a strong point of view, I feel like it's backed up with tons of interviews and a lot of data. Telling the right story is really important to me.

Maya: *What have you learned about yourself during your years in journalism?*
Emily: I've learned that I'm very curious and I won't stop until I get to the truth. You know, one of the qualities of a good journalist is to be a little skeptical of the answers and push back when it's necessary. I feel like I've developed a pretty good

instinct for when I'm getting a real story and that's a quality that all journalists need to know. Lately, the media, and as we've seen with the coverage of President Trump, plays a really important role in continuing to be essentially the fourth branch of government. I'm sure the public knows the truth, and I'm just one part of that.

Maya: *Not many people know about what goes behind the scenes in the newsroom. Do you have any special routines that you like to do just before going on air?*

Emily: I like to be prepared, so I make sure I've reviewed all the stories and I'd come up along with my team with what I hope will be compelling questions. But sometimes, I also think preparing too much doesn't lead to the best results. You have to let things unfold on air. And so, finding that balance of preparation, but also being able to be spontaneous.

Maya: *What is your advice that you would give to young journalists?*

Emily: I think this is one of the most important jobs in the world, getting to the truth. Journalism is a really worthy career and you get to learn so much so fast that you will never be bored. It's an industry that I would encourage anyone to explore because I've learned so much myself.

Maya: *You were ranked 10th on the 100 most influential tech woman on Twitter by Business Insider. How does that feel and what does that mean to you?*

Emily: You know it's always nice to get recognition. There are some incredible journalists out there covering technology and incredible women in technology and I learned so much from many of them. I've had the opportunity to get to know some of them over the course of my career. I'm so proud of what women in the industry are doing to do their own part to change the world but also break down some of the walls that have prevented women from shattering that silicon ceiling. So, I hope to see much more in years to come.

Ilana Stern

Founder, Weddington Way

Ilana Stern is the founder and former CEO of the start-up Weddington Way, a company that is a digitalized fashion brand which focuses on making a personalized shopping experience for customers during their special occasions, which was bought by Gap Inc. Prior to her start-up, Stern was an entrepreneurship lecturer at Stanford Graduate School of Business and later became a buyer for the company Bloomingdale's in New York. She received her MBA from Stanford Graduate School of Business and graduated summa cum laude from the University of Pennsylvania.

Maya: *What motivated you to start your own company?*
Ilana: I started working on my company Weddington Way when I was in business school at Stanford. I was just sort of tinkering with ideas and I wasn't sure if I was going to start a company or join a company. Ultimately, the number one reason that really drew me in was the opportunity to solve an acute consumer pain. It was by observing amongst my peers, a lot of challenges and trouble around shopping for special

occasions and that actually intrigued and pulled me into this field. And realizing that there weren't any good solutions out there, especially for the millennial generation and younger generations based on how we are used to shopping by consuming media is definitely very different from other generations. So, the primary motivator for starting my company was solving a consumer pain point.

Maya: *What was in your education or your previous work that helped you to become a CEO?*
Ilana: It's funny because there's no one bullet rather it's actually a lot of little steps along the way that helped me become a leader. I was fortunate enough to have two very supportive parents who prioritized education and I was always very self-motivated in terms of working hard in school and trying to get good grades. A lot of it was internal motivation from me; I've always been competitive against myself and not other people. In the early days, it was a lot of learning, thinking about high school and college, learning how to really focus and how to prioritize and synthesize cross functionally. Being a CEO requires you to synthesize information and from a lot of different places and think about very different problems. One day it might be a finance or a funding problem and another day, it might be a customer problem or a team problem. For me, having a liberal arts education where you are doing cross functional work, helped, and then my first job out of college I was a buyer for Bloomingdale. It was not a very traditional path coming out of Penn and Wharton Business School because there were lots of people going into management, consulting and finance research paths.

For me, going into retail and taking that path was very

untraditional, but it was a really great experience. I had a lot of responsibility from immediately out of college in terms of owning a P&L which stands for profit and loss. I also went to Stanford Business School, and what was really great about that business school was I spent a lot of my time stepping outside my comfort zone. I am a firm believer that we can be taking risk to get better at something. I always took a lot of opportunities to pitch the startup idea I was working on. I just did things that were new to me and I think I got better at doing that as I progressed through my career and that is a huge part of being a CEO and a leader.

Maya: *What leadership principles helped you go through good and bad times?*
Ilana: Authenticity or staying true to yourself has been something that is really important for me. What I mean by authenticity is that I feel really lucky that while I was growing up, I was super focused getting good grades and on my track to college. My parents were a really good reminder that I needed to spend time doing things I love and not just do things to build up my resume that would help me get into college. It helped me focus my energy and time on doing things that I loved. And they also showed me that trying out new things was very important and if I don't like them that was okay. There might have been things that I would have done to try to make myself look better for college that just weren't actually authentic to me and something that I would personally feel really passionate about.

As a leader of a startup, you don't have much, so, values form an important part of who you are. You've got whatever funding you've managed to scrape together, and you go through good times and bad. The main glue that holds a team together and a company together is culture and its values. That has been one of our really important values at Weddington Way. Our values were warmth, compassion and empowerment. Warmth and compassion because that's how we wanted to make each other feel. We have created a strong community where we prioritize the human first and we really had each other's back. One time, we had one employee who was diagnosed with cancer after she delivered her second baby; she was on leave indefinitely and the team just sort of pulled together and covered her work. A bunch of us would rotate and pick her up and driver her to chemotherapy in the middle of the week.

Empowerment was always a really important value because we just had a lot of smart and hungry people coming into the company and taking ownership of something they knew how to do. Some folks were just figuring things out and we found out when we give people leeway to try new things and make mistakes and figure stuff out, they found their path to what they were great at and helped the company achieve great things. So those are a few things that are very core to what helped us get through the bad times and what made the good times feel so good.

Maya: *Especially with AI expansion just around the corner, does technology help or hinder you getting things done for your company in general.*
Ilana: I mean, so our company Weddington Way was very much technology enabled company, a social commerce site where my friends could shop together no matter where they lived which is a hugely tech enabled experience. We leveraged data about what people were shopping for and how they were

Stepping outside of your comfort zone is something that you can practice and get better at. So, I would advise basically anyone at any age to just continuously try to do things that are outside your comfort zone and push the limits of what is possible for you.

shopping to make the experience that they were having with our brand more personal to them. From a personal perspective, technology in some ways can be hugely empowering and other times it can be a total hindering scene. We can spend way too much time cleaning our inbox or on social media.

Maya: *What advice you would give to someone who is just starting out or trying to start a business or maybe they're in high school and they want to be in the business field?*
Ilana: I would have few pieces of advice. Stepping outside of your comfort zone is something that you can practice and get better at. So, I would advise basically anyone at any age to just continuously try to do things that are outside your comfort zone and push the limits of what is possible for you. No matter what task you take, I think you should always improve your confidence and your awareness of the balance of what's possible for you, which will be greater than you originally thought.

Also, I think it's our society can often promote showing confidence to the point of arrogance. I actually think a really confident thing to do is show vulnerability and have the humility to say when you don't know the answers to something, or you don't know how to do something. That is the path to actually learning a lot more and becoming a much stronger businessperson, leader, or whatever you're going after.

Lastly, it's really helpful when you think you might want to go down a certain path, to talk to a lot of people who have gone down that same path and are further down the road than you are. Try to learn and understand what they like about what they're doing, understand what they don't like and that'll help you form your intuition as to what type of work will make you happy and excited to do every day.

Jacinda Ardern

Prime Minister, New Zealand

Jacinda Ardern is the 40th Prime Minister of New Zealand. She graduated from the University of Waikato with a Bachelor of Communication Studies in Politics and Public Relations. Post-university, she worked as an advisor in the office of then-Prime Minister Helen Clark, in London, for the Government Cabinet Office and as an Assistant Director in the Department for Business and Enterprise, and on a review of Policing in England and Wales. The Prime Minister joined the New Zealand Labour Party at age 18 and entered New Zealand's Parliament in 2008. Over her nine years as a representative, she has been a strong advocate for children, women, and the right of every New Zealander to have meaningful work. She became the MP for the Auckland electorate Mt. Albert in early 2017, and the Leader of the Labour Party in August 2017. In addition to being the Prime Minister, she holds the roles of Minister for National Security and Intelligence, Minister for Arts, Culture and Heritage, and Minister for Child Poverty Reduction, an issue particularly close to her heart.

Maya: *You are the youngest woman in the world to lead a country. How do you see your role as a leader for not only New Zealand but also for girls around the world who aspire to be leaders?*

Jacinda: I try and be the best leader I can for New Zealand. If that means a few other young women or girls decide to be leaders — then that's fantastic!

Maya: *When did you know that you wanted to go into politics and serve the country?*

Jacinda: I always knew being a member of parliament was a great job — I just didn't necessarily believe I would be one; I'm glad I took the opportunities when they came along.

Maya: *What do you think has changed in the way you govern now after giving birth to your daughter?*

Jacinda: I try now to get home to give her a bath and put her to bed!

Maya: *Given the current global and national problems our world is experiencing such as gun violence, immigration crisis, rise of nationalism, economic competition and more, does the solution lie in globalism or nationalism or a blend of both? How do you think about these issues?*

Jacinda: We can be both proud of who our countries are, and the values we have, while also be open and focused on solving the world's problems, collectively the world has become quite binary — the key is to remember our humanity.

Evidence based decision making, kindness and empathy, and the principle of guardianship that we have to hand this world over to the next generation.

Maya: *The world witnessed your courageous and empathetic leadership during a national crisis. What's your source of inspiration and strength? How do you get such moral clarity of thought?*

Jacinda: For me, there is a real simplicity in remembering that we are all humans who experience pain, grief, and hope in the same way. That brings everything into stark relief.

Maya: *It is clear that kindness is a core leadership tenet for you.? What other leadership principles do you live by?*

Jacinda: Evidence based decision making, kindness and empathy, and the principle of guardianship that we have to hand this world over to the next generation.

Maya: I *had a chance to visit New Zealand and the Pacific Islands and I was struck by the impact climate change is already having on the region. How do we come together as nations to solve this urgent crisis?*

Jacinda: Multilateral institutions and instruments are key — we need global goals, rules and a sense of responsibility.

Dr. Janet Yellen

Former Chair of the Federal Reserve

Dr. Janet Yellen is an economist who was the former Chair of the Board of Governors of the Federal Reserve System. Yellen became the first female to hold this position. Previously, she had also served as Vice Chair as well as President and Chief Executive Officer of the Federal Reserve Bank of San Francisco. Yellen graduated summa cum laude from Brown University with a degree in economics in 1967. She received her doctorate in economics from Yale University in 1971. From 1971 to 1976, she was an assistant professor at Harvard University. From 1977 to 1978, she worked for the Board of Governors as an economist, before joining the faculty of the London School of Economics and Political Science (1978–80). Yellen is currently at the Brookings Institution along with her predecessor, former Federal Reserve Chair Ben Bernanke working with the Hutchins Center on Fiscal and Monetary Policy. She has received a number of academic honors during her career. These include the Wilbur Cross Medal from Yale in 1997, an honorary doctor of laws degree from Brown in 1998, and an honorary doctor of humane letters from Bard College in 2000.

Maya: *What did you want to be as a child?*

Janet: Well, I liked math very much in high school and also liked science. I had a wide range of interests. I took a lot of science in high school and when I went to college, I was exploring math and chemistry as areas that I might major in. When I discovered economics, which was in my freshman year, I really loved it because it was very mathematical, but it was also about human welfare, issues that touch everybody's lives and have a lot to do with whether or not people feel happy and fulfilled. I was drawn to the combination of rigorous thinking that uses analytic tools, including math and had applicability to different areas.

Maya: *How did it feel to serve as the first female Federal Chair? What message do you think it carries for young women around the world?*

Janet: Well, you know, I worked my way up in the ranks. I had been president of the Federal Reserve Bank of San Francisco, I had been a governor in the 1990s, I was Vice Chair before I was chair and so I had a lot of experience and it fit very well. To me, when I was first appointed, it felt like, 'ok, this is a slightly higher position', but I was vice chair — which is the number two position — so I thought I had only been promoted. It's only one step, I thought, and I felt pretty well prepared to take on the job with my past experience.

What I quickly discovered, was that to the outside world, and particularly to young women it was a huge deal and they did not regard it as, 'oh, you've got promoted and you've been doing this all along'. I encountered many young women who seemed to be very inspired by the fact that I reached the top and so in that sense, I'd broken the glass ceiling. It was much more visible to them and over the four years that I did that, I had the chance to meet with many young women, including women who majored in economics or finance; women who were interested in going on to graduate school; women who were working in companies on Wall Street who I think feel inspired to the woman working in quantitative fields that are dominated by men. I do think it means a lot to women and they appreciated seeing a woman being able to do all that the job entails. It has a more important public role on TV or testifying before Congress in visibly high-pressure situations. I think they feel proud that a woman could get to the top and I felt that way too, especially when I saw what their reaction was.

Maya: *What have you learned about yourself during your years as serving as the Federal Chair?*

Janet: I focused a lot on leadership, and on trying to inspire the people that I worked with, to feel good about their jobs, to feel devoted to it and proud of what they were doing. I learned that I had the capacity to motivate people to understand the importance of what they were doing, and to feel a sense of devotion and loyalty to the Federal Reserve and to its mission as well as to feel part of a team. Even in the decision-making process, the committee that makes monetary policy (which is called the Federal Open Market Committee and has 19 people on it including the presidents of the Reserve Banks, and the seven governors) come from different walks of life — different backgrounds, different parts of the country, and different political views and affiliations. I recognized that it was very important to make an institution like that and the way to do is to make the people feel part of a group that they care about one another and the success of the group and are willing to subjugate their personal desire to stand out or get famous or get attention to the success of a common cause. I'm just pleased that I could work with people from different backgrounds, in a nonpolitical, nonpartisan spirit, debate things, showing respect for one another and create a sense of collegiality.

Maya: *Were there any struggles on your path to becoming the first female Federal Chair?*

Janet: Well, it's very hard to become the Federal Chair, and it's something that would be hard to aspire to because it would be like being president of the United States in a sense that very few people will get to do it. There are many people who are potentially qualified for it and in a way, you have to be lucky and I did recognize that there had never been a female Federal Chair and finance is a man's world. I knew that I would be fighting a perception that you can't trust women. For example, this perception of that if there was a crisis you would need a man to be able to deal with it as they have the toughness to manage. When I was being considered, there was a lot of discussion in the newspaper, and those views did surface, so I regarded that as sexism. I realized those views are out there. In that sense, it's tough to get selected. I was very pleased and lucky that President Obama decided to choose me.

Maya: *Aside from your life in economics, what are some of your hobbies?*

Janet: I like to read, travel, and cook. I really enjoy eating out; I'm a little bit of a foodie. I also like hanging out with my family.

First of all, study hard, take your work seriously, and find something to do that you really enjoy — that is really important. Don't get locked in too early. Look at a lot of different things. Let yourself discover what you love. Getting to the top isn't that important, I would say. I was lucky enough to get to the top, but what is important is having something to do with your life.

Maya: *Who is someone you looked up to as a mentor throughout your life and what advice did they give you?*

Janet: I had a very important mentor when I was a student studying economics, his name was James Tobin and he was a Nobel Prize winner who had served on the Council of Economic Advisers under President Kennedy. He was famous for the contributions made in economics and economic policy. He was a really inspiring figure to me. He took economics very seriously and felt it as the greatest importance and that mattered to people in their lives. That's what economists should be focused on — the impact of economic policy on the well-being of people and that it could make a big contribution to the economic policy. He really supported me throughout my entire career and so he was important to me. The other person who had an impact on me was my spouse, also an economist and ended up winning the Nobel Prize. He and I worked together, we wrote papers together, we did research together as well while being married, having a son who has gone into economics. Having a husband who has always been supportive of my career, who is and is always willing to make sure that I got to do the things that would facilitate my success. He has moved with me on several occasions to Washington and been willing to organize our joint lives so that I would have these opportunities. So, I'd say, he has also been a mentor to me.

Maya: *What advice would you give to girls who want to follow your footsteps?*

Janet: First of all, study hard, take your work seriously, and find something to do that you really enjoy — that is really important. Don't get locked in too early. Look at a lot of different things. Let yourself discover what you love. Getting to the top isn't that important, I would say. I was lucky enough to get to the top, but what is important is having something to do with your life. Assuming that you are going to work, a career that you really enjoy and you feel the work is meaningful, you want to get up to every day, what you're doing is interesting, and you work in an organization where you think they have a mission that you are supportive of the people that you're working with that's what is really important. If you never get to the top positions, it doesn't matter. What matters is that every day you get up and you feel you have something meaningful. So, my advice is to try to figure out what you really enjoy and go for it. Then, work hard and give it your all.

Maya: *What is your view on globalization? Is it net positive for everyone? Or are there winners and losers?*
Janet: There are winners and losers. I think for a country if you add up all the winners and losers, it's a net positive, but they're definitely been losers. We've not done very much to help the losers. Just saying globalization is good, is really not taking the fact seriously, that there are people who lose from it. I think that's something we should have paid much more attention to. Now, we're hearing a lot from the losers who were letting everybody know how much they've suffered from globalization. I would say globalization is a part of what's happened to hold down wages for reasonable share for the workforce. More importantly than that is the nature of technological change, the kinds of inventions and technological developments we've had, have consistently raised the demands for skills and benefited people who have more skills particularly college education and harm to people

who have less skill. When you think about manufacturing jobs, for example, President Trump shows the fact that there's been a loss of those jobs and it's partly the Chinese and others that are making goods and services and selling them to us that once upon a time we made here. But much more important than that is the fact that if you go to a factory these days, is now filled with robots. And there are a few people there, but they're sitting on computer consoles. The technology has just taken a lot of the jobs and enabled machines and computers to do them. What we should be doing is retraining people or making sure to get the kind of training that would let them try new things in that kind of environment. And we haven't done that.

Maya: *What is your view on the rise of automation, AI, and robotics on employment? And can this change be managed through policy?*
Janet: I think that's a serious concern, because it's the type of thing that I just mentioned, of technological change that is going to very likely benefit people with skills who can occupy those roles. It will create new jobs, but the jobs it creates are likely to be for people who can manage the robots, program the robot, and take advantage of the technology that they will offer. And it's likely to harm people like say, truck drivers who may be replaced by autonomous driving vehicles and, you know, the Fed and economist generally know how to create, in some sense, enough jobs in the economy; I'm not worried that there won't be enough jobs, but they may not be the kinds of jobs that people wanted, or expected, or hope to get. They may not be in the places that people want them and may not pay the wages that they aspire to. And so, technological change generally makes good things possible. But again, they're

126

always losers. And I fear that the people who lose will be the same people who lost from globalization and all the things we're talking about. There are policies that can help improve things, but it will be challenging; I don't want to minimize the difficulties. There were things we could have done all along all these years with policy and didn't do, as such the consequences that we now have is that there is enormous resistance to globalization. So, I don't want to say it will be easy to deal with the consequences of those.

Maya: *How do you feel about leaving the economy stronger than you found it? And what set of policies do you think were critical in shaping the US and global economy?*

Janet: Well, we had a horrific financial crisis in 2008. The policies that were put in place then, were aggressive, inventive, and forceful. It took a very long time to really recover from that crisis. We had to stick with policies that were unconventional and not always very well understood. But I think in the end they were effective, and they lead to the United States being in the good shape that I think it's in now. We had about the lowest unemployment rate in 20 years and quite a strong job market in general, but of course, you know there are a lot of people who are getting low wages, working very hard and doing multiple jobs. But I think the policies that were put in place between 2008 and 2013 or 14 made an enormous difference to where we are. And nothing gives me greater pleasure than the fact that the US economy so thoroughly recovered from that crisis.

Jenny Durkan

Seattle Mayor

When Jenny Durkan won the Seattle Mayoral race, she made history. She became the 56th Mayor of Seattle and the first woman to lead the city in nearly a century. Prior to becoming mayor, Durkan was a civic leader and nationally recognized attorney. From 2009 to 2014, she served as the U.S. Attorney for the Western District of Washington, becoming the first openly gay U.S. Attorney in our country's history. She was a founding board member of the Center for Women and Democracy and trained women running for office in Morocco. She was the first citizen observer on Seattle Police Department's Firearms Review Board and served on two blue-ribbon committees pushing for reforms at SPD. She graduated from the University of Notre Dame, taught school and coached girls' basketball in a Yupik fishing village in Alaska, and then earned her J.D. at the University of Washington School of Law.

Maya: *What were the factors that motivated you to run for office?*
Jenny: I ran for office because I believe I can make a difference. Seattle is amid a crushing affordability crisis that

has left far too many people behind. Our most critical issue is homelessness, and as a city with so much prosperity, I know that we can do more to move our unsheltered neighbors into secure housing.

Maya: *You became the first female mayor of Seattle in almost 100 years. What does that mean to you? What does that say about our country?*

Jenny: It is a great opportunity to serve as your Mayor; but with the honor comes a deep responsibility. When you add diversity in the workforce, one of the things you are doing is bringing different points of view and so if you bring a woman into a position where usually men have done it, you're going to get different points of view; I think we've got to build a very vibrant quilt here — my mayor's office is going to reflect all the people of Seattle.

The election wins we've seen since November 7th are very personal to me for many reasons, creating a pathway for women in leadership is an issue I've championed for decades; I taught women in the Middle East how to run for office after 9/11, and I served on the board of the Center for Women and Democracy. This election is the beginning of a dream realized for that organization and many other organizations that have fought to level the playing field for women entering into elected office. I think it's remarkable that in less than one year after the Women's March — the largest single-day demonstrations around the globe, in history — when you look at the political landscape, you see a diverse wave of women coming into power across the US! Despite the challenges, women are making a difference. Women of color, gay women, trans women, all women, are rising to prominence.

Maya: *Whenever I am in downtown Seattle, the homelessness everywhere makes me feel sad. What can the government do about it? What can the citizens do about it?*

Jenny: We are facing unprecedented challenges as a city and we need innovative solutions to help move those experiencing homelessness into stable, affordable housing. One really important factor in addressing this crisis is that people are finally acknowledging that homelessness is as big a problem as it is. Now, we need to reframe the way we have been trying to address homelessness — it's not a one-size fits all problem. We need a myriad of voices at the table to provide answers and make sure we are making decisions that will provide immediate relief for our communities. Before taking the oath of office, I assembled a 61-member transition team full of community members and policy experts who would make key, achievable policy recommendations that could make a difference in the short-term on our homelessness crisis. In my first action as mayor, I signed an Executive Order aimed at quickly developing and implementing strategies to assist rent-burdened lower income households pay for their housing. But government cannot solve this problem alone; we need a unified collaborative effort that must involve everyone in this fight: service providers, caring philanthropists, communities, individuals and businesses dedicated to finding innovative long-term housing solutions. I've been heartened by how much will there is in every sector of the city to do something in the area of homelessness and how much people want it to be better. I think getting that kind of political will is always the first step and it's no doubt that we have it.

Be engaged as early as you can and as often as you can. Don't be afraid to fall or fail, that means you are pushing yourself and you always learn something!

Maya: *What role do you see for Seattle in a global economy?*
Jenny: We are the city that invents the future — and we will continue to look to the horizon and create that better future. But first, to remain a global leader, we must tackle our issues of affordability that limit our young people from reaching their full potential. That's why, in another early move, I signed an Executive Order creating the framework to extend the Seattle Promise free college tuition program from one year of free college to two years for Seattle public high school graduates. The City of Seattle must play an active role in reducing and removing financial barriers that keep our high school graduates from going to college or getting the technical training they need. This will not just be good for our students; it will be great for Seattle. It will help channel the prosperity of our thriving economy back into our community and let us start filling thousands of job openings with our home-grown talent.

Technology can be at the center of solutions for our most critical challenges — as we reframe the way in which we are addressing our homelessness crisis, as we strive to be a more inclusive city, as we develop and implement green technology strategies — Seattle will continue to be a global leader at the forefront of innovation.

Maya: *What advice would you give your younger self?*
Jenny: Be engaged as early as you can and as often as you can. Don't be afraid to fall or fail, that means you are pushing yourself and you always learn something!

Dr. Jocelyn Bell Burnell

Astrophysicist and Professor

Dr. Jocelyn Bell Burnell is an astrophysicist from Northern Ireland. She studied at the University of Glasgow graduating with a Bachelor of Science degree in Physics and received her PhD degree from the University of Cambridge. Burnell discovered the first radio pulsars in 1967. She was credited with "one of the most significant scientific achievements of the 20th century." The discovery was recognized by the award of the 1974 Nobel Prize in Physics, but despite being the first to observe the pulsars, she was not one of the recipients of the prize. In 2018, Burnell was awarded the Special Breakthrough Prize in Fundamental Physics. She donated the entire prize money to help female, minority, and refugee students become physics researchers.

Maya: *When did you realize you had interest in science and, more specifically, in physics and astronomy?*
Jocelyn: As soon as we started doing science in school (at age 12), it was clear that I was good at physics, OK at chemistry, but not interested in biology. I continued to be good at physics all the way through my school years — and also pretty good

I hope lots of girls will go for careers in science, technology, and computing etc. They are all great areas to work in and society needs people in these areas. Girls are often more thoughtful and careful, so they are especially useful in such domains.

at math, and so it looked as if I would become a physicist. I was wondering what kind of physics I would do ultimately (physics sets one up for a wide range of careers), but when I read some astronomy books from the local public library (at about age 15), I realized that I would love to be an astronomer. As I learned more about astronomy, I became particularly interested in radio astronomy (looking at the stars and galaxies through the radio waves they emitted).

Maya: *Did you ever doubt yourself when you were taking physics at the University of Cambridge?*

Jocelyn: I wonder if you have ever heard of 'imposter syndrome'? You can probably find out about it on Google if you have not already heard of it. Looking back on my time in Cambridge, I can see that I was suffering from imposter syndrome. I was sure that everyone else was much cleverer than me, that they had made a mistake giving me a place at Cambridge, that they would soon discover their mistake and throw me out of Cambridge. I decided I would work my very hardest so that when they threw me out, I would not have a guilty conscience — I simply was not bright enough for Cambridge. So, I was working very hard and very thoroughly because I doubted my abilities.

Maya: *What advice do you have for young girls who want to pursue science and computing?*

Jocelyn: I hope lots of girls will go for careers in science, technology, and computing etc. They are all great areas to work in and society needs people in these areas. Girls are often more thoughtful and careful, so they are especially useful in such domains.

Maya: *How does society need to change to help girls and women pursue STEM fields and careers?*

Jocelyn: Gradually, society is realizing that some of the practices we have disadvantage girls (and some minority groups also) and is taking steps to make things fair for all. A few more steps are still needed, but we are definitely moving along that road. For example, in the UK, we have the Athena SWAN scheme: an organization established to advancing the careers of women in STEMM (STEM+Medicine). And there is more sharing of childcare and domestic jobs between men and women these days.

Some of the 'discrimination' is very subtle — for example, have you ever had to fill out a form and it asks which sex or gender you are? Does it have two boxes and you have to tick one? Which box comes first? And, secondly, I hope that someday soon there will be more than two boxes because we recognize that there are more possibilities than straight female and straight male (but that is opening up a whole new area).

Maya: *I have been fascinated by the question of extraterrestrial life. I was wondering if you have formed a view on the subject. Can we really be alone in this universe?*

Jocelyn: The universe is such a big place and we have come to see that there are lots of planets around many stars, so I suspect that somewhere there will be life out there. But because of the large distances, it may be impossible to be in contact.

Jody Williams

Nobel Laureate in Peace

Jody Williams is an American female political activist known for her efforts on banning anti-personnel landmines, her protection of human rights, and her work to spread awareness of the safety and security in our society. She received the Nobel Peace Prize in 1997 for work in banning and clearing landmines. Since her protests of the Vietnam War, she has been a life-long advocate of freedom, self-determination and human and civil rights. Williams continues to be recognized for her contributions to human rights and global security. She is the recipient of fifteen honorary degrees, among other recognitions. In 2004, Williams was named by Forbes Magazine as one of the 100 most powerful women in the world in the publication of its first such annual list.

Maya: *At what moment in your life did you become an activist? What strategies have worked best for you to get your message across?*
Jody: There were various choices that I made even when I was quite young which moved me along a path ultimately resulting in my activism. For example, defending my handicapped

brother, Steve, when I was young, and later standing up to bullies in grade school. Later, in university, I joined people across the U.S. protesting the country's war in Vietnam. I'd say that by that point, I knew I wanted to be part of positive change in and for our country. However, I didn't use the word "activist" in relation to myself for many years. Strategies that have worked best for me are working in coalitions of organizations and individuals who share the same vision for change. Each person brings their own talents and creativity to the effort that's what makes the overall work broad, strong and vibrant.

Maya: *What does peace mean to you? How are environment and peace related?*

Jody: Peace is not simply the absence of armed conflict. In fact, that is the bare minimum upon which to build sustainable peace. For me, sustainable peaceful society is a world in which the basic needs of all are met: food, drinking water, housing, education, access to medical care, etc. Links between environment and peace are complex. But as we witness changes in the environment, we see people having to move from where they have lived and find new homes, which leads to conflict with those already living there. For example, in areas of Africa where desertification has spread, nomadic people have moved onto lands where farming people live to feed their animals. Obviously, this causes conflict between the groups. Islands in the South Pacific are facing rising waters that will result in the disappearance of the islands. Where will the people living there go now?

Greed and a lust for power,
which lead to gross inequalities,
disregard for human rights, and
human dignity.

Maya: *Who were the role models you looked up to while growing up? Whom do you look up to now?*

Jody: As a kid, I thought Helen Keller was pretty amazing. And Anne Frank. But I'm not sure that constituted looking up to them. The people who inspire me now are not the people most people would know. They are often very poor women around the world working to create peace in the midst of war or seeking justice after wars end. Women in the Democratic Republic of Congo, Guatemala, Rohingya and their families driven into Bangladesh from their homes in Burma/Myanmar.

Maya: *What do you think is the root cause of conflict?*

Jody: Greed and a lust for power, which lead to gross inequalities, disregard for human rights, and human dignity.

Laurie Segall

Journalist and Former Technology Correspondent at CNN

Laurie Segall is a former CNN technology correspondent as well as the producer of the TV series, *Mostly Human*, which explores the different ways in which technology has impacts on sex, love, and death. She was the senior technology correspondent and editor at CNN for more than a decade where she interviewed influential leaders such as Mark Zuckerberg, Tim Cook, Jack Dorsey, and Bill Gates. She graduated with a B.A. in political science at University of Michigan and was later hired to be a full-time news assistant at CNN. Segall has covered national breaking news counting the Boston Marathon bombing, Hurricane Sandy, and Hurricane Irma. At 26, Segall appeared on Forbes "30 Under 30" list in the media category.

Maya: *What motivated or inspired you to pursue a career in journalism?*
Laurie: Ever since I was young, I've always been a storyteller and I've always been very curious about people. I was editor of my school newspaper in high school, and I love telling

different stories or finding stories that people wouldn't have found and then writing about them, so I knew that I wanted to be a journalist.

Maya: *Why did you choose to be a reporter in the tech industry rather than politics, social media, etc.?*
Laurie: When I started covering tech, a lot of the social media was launching. In 2010, I was very interested in the underdogs, people who didn't fit in the lines. At that time, the App Store had launched, the iPhone had come out, and the App Store was the canvas for creativity. We were coming out of the recession and there was a group of people who didn't feel like they needed to go to Wall Street to get jobs. These people were creative and thought they can have an idea, so they put it into the hands of millions of people. Those people, to me, were really inspiring. It was almost as if you were liking the band before the band got cool.

These people ended up being the founders of Instagram and other tech companies that have now grown into the billion-dollar businesses. I got into it just because I was curious about the underdogs, I was curious about the creators, I was curious about people who were creating products and thought they could change the world, as well as people who just didn't fit the usual mold. There were incredibly complicated questions when I started covering tech. It was very much a lot of creative people who had a vision and who didn't quite see the world in a traditional way. They saw the world in the way it could be, and not the way it should be. I was inspired by those people. So that's how I started covering tech.

Maya: *Do you remember your first live report on CNN, and what were some of your takeaways and overall experiences from it?*

Laurie: Yeah, I do. I definitely do. It actually happened by accident; I was not a TV reporter at the time, I was a writer covering technology. A show had seen something I wrote, and they asked me to come on TV to talk about it and I was so nervous! I was waving my hands around because when I get nervous, I wave my hands around like a crazy person [laughs]. I said the phrase, "you know," about 100 times. It was almost like a decade ago. But I got through it and it was painful to look back on it, but I just kept going. I learned in television, the more you're on, the more you can be yourself on air.

Maya: *What do you think are some of the must have traits for journalism?*

Laurie: Being curious and persistent is incredibly important. I think being scrappy is very, very important, as in being willing to not take no for an answer, to pick up the phone and call somebody, to go the hard route and not give up. Also, something that might get lost in the mix is kindness, having a good heart, wanting to do the right thing, wanting to hold people accountable, and take that risk. Being persistent, but not annoying — not taking no for an answer is an example, but also walking that delicate line of not being annoying when you're trying to get an interview is really important as well.

Maya: *How do you think the role of digital and social media in transforming journalism?*

Laurie: The role of digital and social media continues to transform journalism. It's interesting for me because I cover these companies and then these companies disrupted us — the

Oftentimes, we have this narrative that the people who are the most powerful people in the world are invincible and that the story of how these companies were created in a straight line. The truth is none of them happened in a straight line. A lot of these people have dealt with incredible highs and lows and many failures.

media industry. The way we view video, Facebook's impact on video, all the analytics that you now have — it's a double-edged sword. I think it's great in many ways and in other ways, it's just new territory which is constantly changing. Companies that do the best are the ones that are scrappier, trying new things and are entrepreneurial about different approaches. I also think that digital and social media has changed the way we record. You find out about things happening in our world on your Twitter or you track down sources on Instagram. It's a completely different game than when I first started. The digital transformation is shaping the media and social media is playing a very important role in it.

Maya: *After interviewing many CEOs of tech giants, what were some of your favorite interviews and why?*
Laurie: I always like interviews that have a certain amount of humanity in them, where people really feel like themselves. It's funny, because I started interviewing a lot of these CEOs when there were just 4 or 5 people in the company and, now, they're billion-dollar companies. My favorite one was with Evan Williams, who's one of the founders of Twitter. It took him a little bit, but he opened up about what it was like to be fired from Twitter, how it was his darkest moment and how he was able to pick up the pieces. Oftentimes, we have this narrative that the people who are the most powerful people in the world are invincible and that the story of how these companies were created in a straight line. The truth is none of them happened in a straight line. A lot of these people have dealt with incredible highs and lows and many failures.

I've also interviewed Mark Zuckerberg and I think interviewing Mark during some of the tougher times for the company was quite interesting. It was an important interview because it represented his moment in time of the unintended consequences of technology, of this idea that there's been so much innovation, and we've been celebrating tech for many years and there are downsides that we have to pay attention to. When the Cambridge Analytica scandal broke out, a lot of users were deeply offended by the fact that they didn't know what happened to their data. So, sitting across from Mark, at a moment where we all wanted to know where the accountability was, was an important moment for me as a journalist. It's important to challenge the leaders about the human impact of their technology.

Maya: *Do you think AI will serve for the greater good or for the worse for the world? What do you think will happen in the long run with AI?*

Laurie: Artificial intelligence is technology, and technology is a double-edged sword. Technology is neutral, and can be good, and it can be used in bad ways. I think there are a lot of ethical issues and many discussions to be held. AI can be incredible for the workforce, but we need to get ahead of that. We need to be having more ethical conversation about the power of AI and doing so in a human way where people understand the human impact. We need to be having these conversations today and tomorrow. What we run into sometimes, like fake news — which is spreading on Facebook — was a result of AI; algorithms picked up this idea that a lot of people were clicking on certain posts, and so AI optimized for that algorithm. The algorithm made certain posts more popular, so more people see it and it started the destructive cycle of false news spreading virally.

Solutions are always to a degree about humanity which is a human conversation regarding how we treat these algorithms, about what we need to do, and what the impact of having these ethical conversations from the beginning. Hopefully, leaders in Silicon Valley are leading the charge on that, but it's an important one because it is an incredible complex question about the future.

Maya: *Although there are plenty of female journalists, were there any moments in your life that hindered you from becoming who you are today, especially since you report in tech?*

Laurie: Look, I've seen a lot of unconscious bias and a lot of things happen in the tech community that aren't necessarily fair. When I interview people, I do a lot of research and work to really get to know who they are. One time I was doing an interview with a very well-known entrepreneur/investor on the stage. We were out after the interview, and he said something to me about the reason people really liked the interview was because we have sexual chemistry. And that was so unfair. I had this really hard moment as a journalist and I said, "No, it's because I do the hard work, I am well respected in the industry, and I've been covering you guys for about eight years." I deal with it like other women deal with it. It is so important to have each other's back whether you do it publicly or privately. For me, I've helped support other women behind the scenes and other women have helped support me. It's important to support other women in any possible ways you can find. It certainly pays off. Unfortunately, at the end of the day, being a woman covering tech is tough because it is still a boy's industry. You deal with all sorts of sexism, but if anything, it makes me more

153

passionate and driven to tell a story that people who don't have their story told by a true narrative.

Maya: *In your TV series, Mostly Human, you talk about how technology impacts a wide variety of themes such as love, death, humanity and others. Which theme do you think tech impacts the most and why? Does it have a positive or negative effect?*

Laurie: Software is like the fiber of society. I genuinely think that it's impacting all of us in variety of ways. As I said before, tech is neutral. We have to start having some uncomfortable conversations about it. For me, as a journalist, I have to start telling the impact of technology. For my show, I interviewed a woman whose best friend had died, and she collected his text messages and his social media history and used artificial intelligence to create something called a bot. A bot is almost like a computerized version of script that uses all the data it was trained on. This woman basically created a text messaging bot that trained up on the data of her best friend. It was almost like a digital version of her best friend. She would text the Roman bot (his name was Roman), and it would text back very similar to what Roman would have said. One time when she was at a party and texted Roman, she said it was almost like she was texting her dead best friend for an hour. So, there were all these ethical issues for this bot — this bot was trained off of data where it could say things and get it wrong, and they could be perceived as something Roman would say. The bot was a complete mourning tool for people like her, but Roman's mother couldn't have access to it because she couldn't devise a man as a machine. Sometimes she would just think the bot was her son and it wasn't. That's a real genius way to think about AI.

Think about all the content we put out there. You could take all that content and create a digital version of yourself using artificial intelligence. The real question is, if you could, should you? What are the unintended consequences? That's how I like to tell the story. I like to tell the story through the human lens, and with real emotion and showing what's coming down the pipeline, however scary, weird, or interesting it may be. In my experience, it's not just the billionaires and the tech entrepreneurs at the center of it all who are shaping culture, community, and future technologies. It's the people on the fringes, the people on the corners that you don't hear about who are experimenting or doing different things. Those are the stories I love to tell. Technology is now how we date, how we love, how we spend time with our family. It's always through a screen. These are the questions that we as consumers and our tech leaders need to answer because I think it is a really pivotal moment.

Maya: *What are some of the tech trends that you've been tracking?*
Laurie: I think bots are a very interesting influence. When you look at what happened with the election and the unintended consequences with Facebook, data and privacy. Privacy is going to be a huge conversation in the next couple of years as we talk about our right to privacy, how much control we really have, and the intelligence in the future of automation will be really important, I think. Those are two trends that I am particularly excited about, bots and privacy. The way that tech companies are dealing with some of the human questions, mental health, and addiction to technology and also how much

time we're spending on our phones is not something that we are talking about, it's something that the tech companies are beginning to talk.

I interviewed Tim Cook, and Apple just launched an addiction tool where you can track how much time you're spending and try to curb it. I mean, this whole addiction to cellphones is a huge issue. Right now, we are at this pivotal moment where we are wondering how to get in front of this complicated relationship with technology. I've always been an optimist and for me technology has shown incredible power and it's done great things and shaped industries. Right now, is a moment for all of us to take a collective breath and take a look at the future.

Another cool tech trend is voice operating systems, you know like Siri and Alexa in your home. We are letting technology and machines into our lives in a very intimate way and it's going to impact ourselves and our children. It makes us ask the question: where does my privacy go? Do we trust these companies that they're not listening to private conversations we have at home? There are so many interesting questions around the fact that machines are becoming almost an extension of ourselves, and they are in our lives in an intimate way. That's is definitely something we are going to be talking about in a couple of years.

Maya: *There seems to be a lot of discussion from Apple, Facebook and Google about privacy. Given that consumers are being tracked all the time, do you think that the situation with privacy will get better in the future?*
Laurie: It has to. What happened with Facebook was a cautionary tale. Now there's a financial cost for not putting

your user's privacy first and for having vague guidelines. That being said, Facebook is a free product; you don't get anything for free. I certainly think that in the future it's going to be something we have to think about. It could potentially get a little bit better, but I also feel that people are going to forget about it. At some point, we will potentially see government regulation. We're asking ourselves right now, are these tech companies too powerful? It will get better when there's more media pressure on these companies, but these are businesses built around our user data, and that's not going to change.

Maya: *What is one of the most memorable places you visited as a journalist?*

Laurie: Oh man! I've been in San Quentin Prison many times for a program called *The Last Mile*, which was about prisoners learning how to code. That's been interesting. For *Mostly Human*, I interviewed a woman who claimed to be in love with a robot and I attended her engagement party outside of Paris. I've been all over the place! I have done interviews in the virtual world. Some of the most fascinating stories for me are the ones that don't come right to you; you have to go look for them. They're unexpected and they take you all around. I'm thankful that my career and my job has taken me to so many different places and so many strange places. Journalism is a career where you must love what you do.

Maya: *Do you have advice for young girls in general and more specifically for girls who want to be in journalism.*

Laurie: Do everything. Life is a process of elimination. Do every job you can to realize the ones you don't want. We put so much pressure on trying to be perfect and having the perfect solution, when sometimes the perfect solution is the one that's at the end of all of the other stuff that you have to go through to help you get there. There's a great Flannery O'Connor quote, "A story is a way to say something that can't be said any other way, and it takes every word in the story to say what the meaning is." I kind of believe that. I have such a better idea of who I am by realizing what I'm not. So, my advice would be not to strive for perfection, it would be to just go get your hands dirty, stay late, come in early, and be curious.

When I started at CNN doing journalism, I was working in the breaking newsroom, and the person who helped me get a full-time job was an editor. I only knew him because I would sit with him in the cafeteria in my free time and I would watch him edit, because I was curious. A job is sometimes a placeholder for the job you want. Sometimes we make the mistake of thinking you get handed things. My advice for people who want to get into journalism is as your first step would be to get in the door to a news company, or wherever you want to work. That alone takes journalistic skills, which is finding the right people to talk to, getting in the front, being persistent, and having confidence. Be persistent, but not annoying. These are all the traits that make a good journalist. Also not being paralyzed by failure, rejection or fear is important. Sometimes they end up being the best things that happen to you.

Lindsey Vonn

Olympian, Entrepreneur

Lindsey Vonn is a former American World Cup alpine ski racer on the US Ski Team. She has won four World Cup overall championships, something only one other female skier has done. As the first American woman, Vonn won a gold medal during the downhill at the 2010 Winter Olympics at Vancouver. She is one of the 6 women to win the World Cup races in all five parts of alpine skiing and has won 82 World Cup races throughout her accomplished career. Vonn is the most successful and considered the greatest of all skiers. She has created a foundation called Lindsey Vonn Foundation which provides future generations with scholarships and plans for education, sports, and enrichment programs to help them reach their goals.

Maya: *Who would you say was the most inspirational person who helped you get started with your skiing career and helped through the ups and down?*
Lindsey: I wouldn't say there is just one person. My grandfather and father passed down their love for skiing to me. My father was my coach at a young age and he always pushed

*I would tell my younger self
(and, hopefully, she would
listen) that all the setbacks she
faces are driving her to a bigger
goal and that she shouldn't be
discouraged, no matter what is
bringing her down — she will
find her way.*

me to do better and gave me the drive to become a champion, while my entire family has always supported me and made huge sacrifices to get me to where I am. I am grateful for my family and friends who are always there to support me — win or lose.

Maya: *What are some of the moments where leadership characteristics played out in your life?*
Lindsey: Leadership is really important — especially when you gain success. You're the boss of your career, and a lot of people are counting on you. I have to be the one to make the big decisions, for example, to pick skis that are the fastest that I'm most comfortable on, to what line I think is the fastest down the hill, or even what event I go to. I have people helping me make those decisions, but I'm also the one who takes the lead to make the final decision I know is best for me.

Maya: *What's your favorite race and why? Which medal are you most proud of?*
Lindsey: I cherish all my medals and, when I look back on them, I think of what obstacles I was facing in my life and how I was feeling. My favorite race is probably Cortina because I've had a lot of success there. I'm most proud of my gold medal, but my bronze from PyeongChang in South Korea is a close second. Those are medals that I worked so hard to get and my family was there with me.

Maya: *Looking back, what advice would you give to your younger self?*
Lindsey: I would tell my younger self (and, hopefully, she would listen) that all the setbacks she faces are driving her to

a bigger goal and that she shouldn't be discouraged, no matter what is bringing her down — she will find her way.

Maya: *Why was it important for you to start the Lindsey Vonn Foundation?*
Lindsey: I wanted to tell young girls what I wish I had told myself when I was young. I want them to have the confidence to be who they want to me. I (hopefully) have paved a path for women in sports, but that's not enough. I want to give girls the tools they need to become empowered, brave, successful women.

Maya: *How do you deal with criticism from social media or otherwise?*
Lindsey: Criticism on social media was very difficult at first. Obviously, it's very personal; you're being personally attacked by someone who doesn't know you, your story, or who you are. I learned to stop looking at comments — good or bad. And if you do read something negative, you have to laugh at it. Laugh at yourself and sympathize for that person who probably has some problems him/herself.

Maya: *Can you give a word of advice to girls who want to be like you?*
Lindsey: I would tell them: "Don't be like me—be like YOU!" If I have a quality you like—of course, use it; if you like skiing—of course, ski. But be your own person and be proud of it!

Maria Cantwell

United States Senator, Washington

Maria Cantwell currently serves as a United States Senator for the State of Washington. As a respected leader — both in public service and in the private sector — Cantwell has always embraced the values she first learned growing up in a strong working-class family. With the help of Pell Grants, Cantwell was the first member of her family to graduate college. Later, as a successful businesswoman in Washington's hi-tech industry, she helped build a company that created hundreds of high-paying jobs from the ground up. Cantwell was elected to the U.S. Senate in 2000, 2006, 2012, and again in 2018, pledging to honor the hard work, aspirations and faith of the people of Washington state. She is working to create affordable opportunities for consumers, businesses and families to make our nation more secure today, to foster innovation for tomorrow, and to stand with parents as they educate and care for their children.

Maya: *According to The Washington Post, the United States is ranked 25th in science literacy and 24th in reading literacy. Given that we compete in a global economy, what are some* *ways to ensure that our education system, especially elementary and high schools, in our state of WA are at par with other nations?*

Maria: You will be pleased to learn that one of my top education priorities as a U.S. Senator has been to support investments in science, technology, engineering, and math (STEM) education. While Washington is a national leader in STEM fields, our state is at serious risk for a workforce shortage in many STEM fields. Washington ranks 46th in the nation when it comes to participation in science and engineering graduate programs. The shortage of individuals with the required skills for these jobs is growing fast. In this Congress, as in the past, I have been a strong supporter of legislation to support partnerships between schools, businesses, universities, and non-profit organizations to support student achievement and teacher training in STEM subjects. Throughout my career, I've fought to bolster STEM programs in Washington state and around the country. Unfortunately, young women and people of color are especially underrepresented in STEM fields. I strongly support legislation to support partnerships between schools, businesses, universities, and non-profit organizations to support student achievement and teacher training in STEM subjects. In the current Congress, I am a cosponsor of S. 1270, the STEM Opportunities Act of 2017, which is focused on creating a more diverse and inclusive STEM workforce. In 2015, I cosponsored S. 1 183, The STEM Gateways Act, which provides grants for elementary and secondary school STEM programs for women and girls, underrepresented minorities, and individuals from all economic backgrounds.

Climate change puts the health, safety, and livelihoods of many Americans at risk. We need to take the risks very seriously and start doing things that will help us come up with better strategies to address this issue.

Maya: *STEM education is important for not only to boys, but girls too. What are your plans to encourage and provide STEM education to girls?*

Maria: It may interest you to know that I am a co-sponsor of federal, comprehensive non-discrimination legislation called the Equality Act (S. 1006). This legislation would expand federal protections to prohibit discrimination on the basis of sexual orientation and gender identity in employment, housing, public accommodations, education, credit, jury service, and receipt of federal financial assistance. This bill was introduced on May 2, 2017 and was referred to the Senate Judiciary Committee, where it currently awaits further consideration.

Maya: *I was recently in the Pacific Islands and found out that some of the islands are sinking due to rising water-levels. It seems like global warming is already having bad impact on the environment. Can this trend be reversed?*

Maria: The issue of climate change is becoming an urgent one every day. As you noticed in your travels, climate change is already impacting our environment. We are seeing these impacts right now in Washington state; it is altering our region's water cycle, threatening drinking water supplies, wildlife and salmon habitat, and the availability of clean and affordable renewable energy. Climate change puts the health, safety, and livelihoods of many Americans at risk. We need to take the risks very seriously and start doing things that will help us come up with better strategies to address this issue. In the wake of the recent natural disasters, I requested the Government Accountability Office to estimate the economic losses from this year's extreme weather events. Based on that report, the consequences of climate change to our economy are estimated to be more than $300 billion in response to severe weather events. We cannot ignore the impact of climate change on our public heath, our environment, and our economy. With commitments from the American people, businesses, and the international community, we can all do our fair share to curb the carbon pollution that is driving climate change. We can reduce emissions, develop and use cleaner energy sources, and boost sustainability. Doing so will not only help us fight back against climate change, but also create vital investment and economic opportunities in resilient infrastructure, low-carbon energy, sustainable agriculture, and new technology.

Maya: *You have worked both in private sector and now in public service. How would you describe your journey?*

Maria: I have always embraced the values I first learned growing up in a strong working-class family. With the help of Pell Grants, I was the first member of my family to graduate college. Later, a businesswoman in Washington's hi-tech industry, I helped build a company that created hundreds of high-paying jobs from the ground up. I would encourage any young person with the desire to serve to pursue a career in government. Today's elected officials come from a variety of backgrounds, hold different degrees, and specialize in a diverse range of issues. Some started as very young men and women, barely old enough to run for office, while others did not get elected until they were already parents or grandparents.

Mary Lou Pauly

Mayor of Issaquah, Washington

Mary Lou Pauly was elected to be the mayor of Issaquah (a suburb of Seattle in the state of Washington) in 2016. Prior to being a mayor, Pauly was trained as a civil engineer who dealt with the city's traffic issues, supply of affordable housing, and the preservation of the environment.

Maya: *What inspired you to run for mayor?*
Mary Lou: I moved to Issaquah in the early 90s and started volunteering for the city. Four years ago, I decided to run for city council and after that, last year, I decided to run for the mayor's job. I was familiar with the issues and wanted to take the city in a different direction. I always loved an area of city planning where we decide what is going to be built on the land. I sat on the development commission. When I first moved in, Costco and Target were just getting built. Now, we don't have much land left to develop, most of it is redevelopment on existing land. We have a plan on the valley floor that I approved as a council member that talked about what this neighborhood will look like around I-90 for the next 20 years. Several projects got constructed that I wasn't particularly

happy with and the community members were not happy with. So, I convinced a lot of council members to vote for something called the moratorium where you stop building for a while and talk to the community about the plan. The moratorium will end soon and so I wanted to move from council member to the mayor's job because mayor is the one who takes what the council says and carries it out. So, the council plans and the mayor executes. I wanted to be on the team that gets the job done.

Maya: *How do you prepare for the debate topics?*

Mary Lou: You never know what the questions are going to be, so you have to practice with your friends for two weeks before the debate. You invite your best friends over and each one of them gets to ask you a question. If you stumble or can't answer it to their satisfaction, they ask the question again and again, until they find the answer convincing. I think it takes 10-20 hours of prep work for each debate. By the time you get to the debate, you are feeling pretty comfortable because your friends have asked you all the hard questions. Debates are fun, but if you don't prepare and have to come up with the answers on the spot, they won't be that much fun.

Maya: *You worked for the city council. What are some of the challenges of working on the council of a small city?*

Mary Lou: The biggest challenge is that seven members of the council have never worked together in a collaborative fashion, all coming to the table with different ideas and perspectives, and now they have to work as a team. That's really challenging. Our town never had something called a strategic plan. But now we are going to work on one. I am excited about that. It is going to help a lot.

Maya: *The traffic in Issaquah is a big problem. How do you plan to fix it?*

Mary Lou: I got an article last year from the Chamber of Commerce, it was a newsletter from 1969 talking about the traffic problems in Issaquah. We have always been at the crossroads to get off the highway and to go somewhere else. So, while our town is small, a lot of people drive through the town to get to somewhere else. We have the city of Sammamish north of us that is twice our size and there are 3-4 cities south of us that are growing. The traffic used to be annoying but now it shuts down parts of the town several times a day. I have a few suggestions. I am going to work with the council and the community to come up with a plan that discourages people to pass through our town. The streets need to look like local streets vs. pass-through lanes. Small changes will encourage people to stay on I-90 and get to their destinations faster. For example, smaller streets with two lane highways are carrying more traffic than state highways with four lanes and I think we change that behavior. Small changes like how the lights work around certain intersections or additional parking in downtown while making the streets narrower will help. Downtown should feel like a destination. So, we need to get everyone moving in the same direction.

Maya: *2017 was a big year for women in politics. What do you think motivated women to run for office and what can we do to get more women in politics?*

Mary Lou: Such a great question. I finished high school in 1980 and went to university until 1985. At the time, there was a lot of excitement about equal rights, fair pay for men and

After the last election, I was not pleased with the policies, but I was very excited to participate in the first women's march last year and the best part was how many women found the courage to run for office. By saying that I want to be part of the solution, they added their voice to the conversation.

women, which were inspiring issues at the time. However, during the last ten years, I have been so disappointed at the opportunities for women and just the general progress on many of these issues. I spent ten years at Bellevue Community College in a program called "Expand your Horizons" for middle school girls to get them interested in STEM and watching the trends over the 25 years, but I have been disappointed. There are some capable and bright women who haven't had the opportunity. After the last election, I was not pleased with the policies, but I was very excited to participate in the first women's march last year and the best part was how many women found the courage to run for office. By saying that I want to be part of the solution, they added their voice to the conversation. In our state, we had a record number of women mayors last year. Very exciting.

Maya: *What aspects of your job are you really looking forward to?*
Mary Lou: When you are a council member, you work with the public. When you are a mayor, you have a team. There are 220 people that work for the city and I am really looking forward to getting to know them. I know only 10. The other thing that I am excited about is the strategic plan that we are going to work on. The decisions that we make in the next four years are going to make an impact for many decades.

Patty Murray

United States Senator, Washington

Patty Murray is Washington State's senior senator. She has proved her herself as an effective leader by solving issues on education, transportation, healthcare, women, veteran, and more. Murray served as the first female Chair of the Senate Veterans' Affairs Committee during the 112th Congress prior to serving as the first female Senator of Washington State. She has also served as the first female Chair of the Senate Budget Committee during the 113th Congress.

Maya: *What inspired you to run for senate?*
Patty: I was watching the Clarence Thomas hearings in the Senate Judiciary Committee in 1991 with my daughter at home in Shoreline, and I looked at the group of men grilling Anita Hill about her interactions with Justice Thomas, and I thought "none of these people are asking the questions I would be asking!" And I realized it was because the senators on that Committee simply didn't reflect the true diversity of the people they were supposed to be representing. That night, I went out with some friends and we were talking about the hearing and I said, "Well maybe I shouldn't just yell at the TV

about this, maybe I should run for the Senate and do something about it!"

And my friends and I all laughed for a bit, but then we stopped laughing, and then we got to work. I pulled together the group of moms and dads who stood with me when I first got into politics to fight budget cuts to pre-K programs, and we put together a grassroots campaign and started talking to as many voters as we could. Nobody thought we were going to win — we were being outspent and dismissed — but I felt so strongly that people in Washington State were frustrated with the status quo and looking for a regular person to represent them, a mom who understood them and what their families were going through. So I worked as hard as I could and, against the odds, I won!

Maya: *What did it mean to you to become the first female Senator from our state?*
Patty: The day after I won the election, I thought to myself how important it was that I succeed so that women and girls looking at me would see that this was possible and would know they could follow in my footsteps. There were so few women senators at that time that I knew that if I didn't do well then people wouldn't just look down on me, but it would make it harder for more women to run and win. In fact, I actually heard that from one young woman! I told her she should think about running for office one day, and she looked at me and said, "I'm going to see how you do, and then I'll see if that's something that looks right for me." That was a lot of pressure, but I had an amazing mentor, Senator Barbara Mikulski of Maryland, who helped show me how things got done in the Senate. And the few of us women worked together, we helped

each other, we helped other women run for the Senate to join us — and now there's a whole lot more of us.

Maya: *You graduated from Washington State University (WSU) with a B.A. in physical education and then you were a teacher. Why did you decide to go from a teacher to be the senator and become such an influential voice on so many pressing issues of our times?*

Patty: I like to joke that I learned a whole lot about being a Senator from my time as a preschool teacher — but I think there's a lot of truth to that! I taught kids about sharing, about being considerate to each other, and other important lessons that I wish some other senators could learn. I first got into politics because a preschool program for my kids was cut by the Washington state legislature and I didn't think that was right. So, I packed my kids up in the car and went to Olympia to tell legislators why this program was so important. But when I got there, one of them told me that I couldn't make a difference because I was "just a mom in tennis shoes." I couldn't believe it. Just a mom in tennis shoes? Well, I wasn't going to stand for that. I drove all the way from Olympia to my house steaming mad. And when I got home, I got to work. I called other moms. They called other moms. We got some dads to help too. And then all of us moms and dads — with a whole lot of tennis shoes — held rallies, made calls, called our legislators... and we won! We got the funding back, and we made it clear that legislators should listen to the people they represent.

I have taken those lessons with me into my job every day — from the school board, to the State Senate, to the U.S. Senate: that my job is to be a voice for the people in

Washington State who too often get ignored. That is what drives me to fight so hard for my constituents and my values and it's what drives my passion for getting results for the people who elect me.

Maya: *What accomplishments are you most proud of?*
Patty: I've been proud to work on so many issues that help Washington State families over the years, but I'll just mention a few.

I was proud to work to finally fix the broken No Child Left Behind education law and replace it with the much better Every Student Succeeds Act. I know how important education is to our students, our communities, and our future as a nation — so I was proud to bring the voices of parents, students, teachers, and so many others into the process to finally fix this broken law.

I was also proud to work with an unlikely partner, House Speaker Paul Ryan, on a budget deal in 2013 that prevented another government shutdown and made important investments in education, health care, and middle-class jobs. To me, this was less about getting a perfect deal, and more about doing whatever I could to end the constant crises that Congress was pushing our country into — and this deal helped do that; at least, for a while.

This isn't a bill, but I am proud every day to help bring the voices of my constituents into the legislative process. When I first got to the Senate, I went to the Senate floor to share a story of a friend who was sick to help make a point about the Family Medical Leave Act that was being debated. When I left the Senate floor after my speech, another senator who had been around for a while looked down at me and said,

From a young age, little girls are given dolls while little boys are given building blocks. We must begin to encourage girls to pursue STEM starting in preschool, through to high school, college and beyond. We know diverse voices help spark innovation, so this isn't only good for girls — it's good for STEM overall.

"We don't tell stories in the Senate — we debate policies." Well, I told him that sharing stories about how federal policies affect people in communities across this country was why I ran for office — and I wasn't going to stop! I've been telling stories ever since, and I believe it's such an important part of my job and it helps make sure that regular people in Washington State have more of a voice than they otherwise would.

Maya: *How do you think we can encourage more girls and their families to let them get into STEM education?*
Patty: From a young age, little girls are given dolls while little boys are given building blocks. We must begin to encourage girls to pursue STEM starting in preschool, through to high school, college and beyond. We know diverse voices help spark innovation, so this isn't only good for girls — it's good for STEM overall.

Maya: *There has been a buzz on school shootings which is placing a ton of worry and fear on students and parents. What can we do about this to make sure school is a safe environment for education and fun?*
Patty: There are a number of steps we can take to address the growing number of school shootings, including adopting common sense gun safety reform and hiring more counselors and mental health professionals to ensure our students are living and developing in a safe, supportive environment. As a mother and a grandmother, I think it's outrageous Congress hasn't done more on tackling gun safety policies, but I'm proud to see Washington State continuing to be a leader on this issue with tougher gun laws.

Maya: *Being female in a mostly male dominated society, were there any struggles to get to where you are now? What guiding principles helped you overcome some of these challenges?*

Patty: Absolutely there were struggles. I was called "just a mom in tennis shoes" who couldn't make a difference when I tried to advocate for more education funding. I was dismissed and diminished when I first ran for the Senate. And when I got to the Senate, I was often the only woman in the room — and my ideas were often overlooked or ignored. And I know I'm not alone — I hear so many stories like this, not just from other women in politics, but women in all types of professions and communities.

My guiding principle has been this: I can't let the struggles get me down, I need to use them to motivate me to fight even harder for policies that put women on equal footing with men. When that man told me, I was "'just a mom in tennis shoes'," he was saying that because he wanted that to be true — he wanted moms in tennis shoes to have no say and to just leave it to people like him. But I wasn't going to let that happen! I think moms in tennis shoes, and women wearing any other kind of shoe should have just as much a voice as anyone else. I have a saying that I like to tell people: If someone tells you that you can't do something, it's because they are afraid you actually will. I try to live by that every day, and I tell every woman and girl to do the same.

Maya: *A few years back, I was visiting the Pacific Islands and I found out that some of the islands are sinking because of rising water-levels. What can we do to spread more awareness about the impact of global warming in the US and around the* *world considering many people don't take it seriously?*

Patty: I believe climate change is one of the most pressing challenges of our time. Already, we are seeing the effects in our state, from ocean acidification, to longer and more devastating wildfire seasons. I've fought for legislation in Congress that protects our environment, such as expanding wilderness areas and investing in renewable energy, and I strongly supported the U.S. joining the Paris Climate Accord, though it's been frustrating to see efforts in Congress to combat climate change get derailed by partisan politics in our nation's capital. That's why I'm grateful and so encouraged by many of the young people I meet both in Washington state and in Washington, DC who are leading the charge and sounding the alarm about the urgent need to take action. I believe your generation will be leaders on climate change and I urge everyone to get involved and make a difference. There's no time to waste.

Maya: *How can we get more women in leadership roles, not only in politics, but also in the corporate world?*

Patty: This is so important — we need more women on corporate boards, we need more women in leadership positions in business, and we need more women in politics. There are so many things we need to do on this front, but I'll focus on just one for now: when women succeed, they need to make sure they keep the door wide open behind them. Doing well for ourselves is important, and setting a good example is necessary, but we all need to work to make sure we're offering a hand to those who are a bit behind us and helping them get ahead. Amazing mentors like Senator Barbara Mikulski have helped me so much over the years, and I think we all need to do whatever we can to help the next generation of women and girls to be able to do even more than we were able to.

Maya: *What is the single biggest challenge our country faces and how is our government addressing it?*
Patty: There are so many, but one that I hear about all the time is the instability that so many families are facing more than ever before. From wages that have stagnated, to higher education costs going through the roof, to food, housing, health care, and child care cost increases, to pensions that are eroding across the country, job instability, and so much more — workers and families today just don't have the stability and the means to get ahead that some previous generations have had. There's so much we need to do to address this — this is a massive challenge — so I'm not going to list off the policies that I believe will move us in the right direction. But I am committed to working on this, and I encourage everyone, especially young people who will face the impact of this when they graduate to make their voices heard.

Maya: *I know you must be busy with work, but what do you do for fun? What are some of your hobbies? What's your favorite book?*
Patty: I love reading. I read all kinds of books and it's hard to pick a favorite! I also enjoy fishing, spending time with my family and visiting and exploring all the great places we have in Washington from our national parks, amazing beaches, mountains, arid ecosystems, and more. We are so lucky to live in this great place. And I'm so proud to get to speak out about all of that in the United States Senate.

Pramila Jayapal

US Representative Washington 7th Congressional District

Pramila Jayapal currently serves as a U.S. Representative from the WA's 7th congressional district. She is the first Indian-American woman to serve in the House of Representative. Before entering the electoral politics, Jayapal was a civil rights activist. She is the First Vice Chair of the Congressional Progressive Caucus and serves on both the Judiciary and Budget committees. Her focus is on ensuring income equality; access to education, from early learning to higher education, including debt-free college; expanding Social Security and Medicare; protecting our environment for the next generation; and ensuring immigrant, civil and human rights for all.

Maya: *What inspired you to run for congress?*
Pramila: I have been an activist for 15 years before I decided to run for office. I actually ran for the State Senate in WA first. I ran for Congress because I felt there needed to be more people that represented the issues and the experiences that I came from as a woman of color and as an immigrant. So, I just didn't see enough of us there and I felt like I had to keep explaining too much. I thought maybe I could change the way

The perception that if you are a girl, you are not good in science and math is just wrong. We need to encourage girls at an early age, give tools to educators to think about engaging girls early, funding other programs outside schools so girls can get additional support.

politics are done; have women, people of color, and more young citizens engaged in the democracy. So, many issues that I care about come from the federal level like immigration, tax system, and economic inequality, and I believed I could make a difference and that's why I ran for Congress.

Maya: *Since this topic impacts a number of students like me, what do you plan to do about STEM education for girls?*

Pramila: That has been a big issue and we have way too few girls in STEM, we have way too few women in Congress. I have signed on a whole series of bills that are around STEM education for girls and teaching girls at an early age. The perception that if you are a girl, you are not good in science and math is just wrong. We need to encourage girls at an early age, give tools to educators to think about engaging girls early, funding other programs outside schools so girls can get additional support. Also, much further down the line, we are working with companies to promote diversity in hiring engineers and coders so working up and down the chain to have a comprehensive view of the situation. We need to do all this so that girls like you know that you are good and just as qualified (sometimes more qualified) to be a fantastic mathematician, scientist, engineer or whatever you want to be.

Maya: *You are the first Indian-American in the house of representatives. You came to the US at age 16. Being a woman of color, did you face challenges to be at the position you are in now?*

Pramila: There have been a lot of struggles over the course of my career in almost every job I had until I started my own organization. I was generally the only woman of color or among very few women or very few people of color, so it has always been challenging to be in a room with others and hear comments made as jokes. People won't listen to a woman of color the same way as they would to a white guy saying the exact same thing. It has been challenging to continuously assert yourself and talk about your accomplishments. Research shows that people don't hear people of color and even if they hear them, they don't believe them. They don't respect the viewpoints of a woman of color as they would for a white male.

Maya: *What kind of policies do you think we need to address global warming?*
Pramila: I have introduced a bill in congress called the 100 by 50 bill along with other colleagues in the house and senators like Sen. Merkley from Oregon, Sen. Sanders from Vermont, and Sen. Booker from NJ. It basically says that we need to set aggressive goals for ourselves that by 2050, we need to be on 100 percent renewable energy. We need to look at all the ways that US can be completely on the renewable energy and stop taking fossil fuels from the ground and also, put resources in black and brown communities, and low-income communities. These communities often have to feel the brunt of the climate change, but don't get the resources to deal with it e.g. toxic dumps, or lead and water issues like in Flint, MI. So, they are part of the same issue of providing climate justice to all.

Maya: *School safety has been a big issue for students like me with incidents like Parkland school shooting. What do you plan to do about that? How can we make our communities and schools safer?*

Pramila: I have signed on to a number of bills that will support banning assault rifles and guns with high capacity magazines. I just introduced a bipartisan bill to raise the age to 21 to buy a gun. I am supporting public health research on gun violence as it is a public health crisis. We also have bills around background checks. What I have been focused lately is to help organize with students like you across the country who care about the issue and use the moment where students are leading the country forward on this issue and provide any help I can to the movement. I am not sure if we are at a tipping point, but we are at a turning point where the country has to face up to the fact that it is ridiculous that in the US, millions of guns are being used to hurt people. That just should not be the case.

Maya: *What is your favorite thing to do as a Congresswoman?*
Pramila: My favorite thing to do is to talk to girls and women of color like you and help open up the possibilities that you can do whatever you want to do, that you remember who you are and if you stay true to who you are, you are going to accomplish great things. Never let anyone tell you that you can't do something, or that you are not as good as the next person. I love engaging with people and help them understand why government and democracy are important.

Robin Hauser

Film Director

Robin Hauser is a film director who has made movies about the gender gap and unconscious bias. Hauser is a brilliant and accomplished director as well as producer of award-winning cause-related documentary films. Her previous film *Running for Jim* won 14 awards in 20 film festivals. She speaks on topics such as increasing diversity in computer programming classes and women's rights. As a businesswoman, professional photographer, and social entrepreneur, Hauser is able to use her skill, creative vision, and passion to create her impactful documentary film projects. Her award-winning film, *Code: Debugging the Gender Gap* gives you a deeper understanding for the gender and minority hiring gap amidst software engineers.

Maya: *What inspired you to do your second movie Code: Debugging the Gender Gap?*
Robin: After having the experience of making my first movie, *Running for Jim*, I loved it! So, I decided to do another movie and I wanted to make it about a really important topic and about something that would help us. And so, at the time, my

We also need to get more role models. You've heard the expression, "you cannot be what you cannot see," and so if we don't have any women in leadership positions, then, it's really hard for people and mostly young children to imagine what they could become.

daughter was studying computer science in college. She calls home and she goes, "Mom, it's weird. There's only one other girl in my class. I don't feel like I belong there," and I was really curious as to what was happening because it seemed funny to me that in a field like computer science where there was such a need for trained students; I mean, we have a big shortage of computer scientists and software engineers, and I felt as though they should be encouraging more people to enter the field. I couldn't understand why more women weren't studying it. So, I started to look into the subject.

Maya: *There's a huge gender gap, as you suggested in the movie, which is hindering girls to be in these kinds of fields. After producing the film, what were your personal takeaways?*
Robin: My biggest takeaway was that it's a very complicated issue — it's not just one thing. But I think we certainly can say that it's a deeply embedded stereotype, and the societal messaging really is teaching our young girls and young women that programming in software engineering and science in general is something that's for boys and for men, and not for girls. I think that Hollywood has a role to play here. The more we get films, movies, TV shows, and gaming with young women featured as being the rock stars will really help. We're not there yet. We need to change societal messaging and to try to change the stereotype. In order to change a stereotype, it takes a long time—about a generation or so. We also need to get more role models. You've heard the expression, "you cannot be what you cannot see," and so if we don't have any women in leadership positions, then, it's really hard for people and mostly young children to imagine what they could become. Then, of course, we have to improve the culture and

workplace environment for women. When you are the minority in a startup vs. tech in general, we have to make it a welcoming space for women. That way, we can retain them into the workforce.

Maya: *In your TED talk, you talked about AI helping to eliminate biases which can sometimes lead to a disaster if it makes a mistake. How do you think that this message should be spread that AI is not the solution to completely eliminating biases around society?*

Robin: People do need to know that. We are using AI in courtrooms, and there are algorithms that help the judge decide who gets to go to jail, but sometimes it makes mistakes because of the bias it was created on. These predictive algorithms that are being used in the courtrooms aren't making decisions, but judges do use them to help make final decisions. That is what's risky. If you do end up having a judge that relies on that type of predictive software, it could be dangerous, because it could be giving them the wrong impression and the wrong data. Doing a TED talk on the subject is a start, and I do know that there are a lot of articles being written about this all the time. The real question is, "who is overseeing the ethical standards of artificial intelligence?" As AI becomes more and more prevalent in our world, and in our society, we need to talk about who is overseeing it, and who is regulating this. I'm not a big proponent of regulations but we regulate the drugs, we don't just let drugs out there that haven't been well tested on people, so then why should it be different with products that might not only offend people, but can actually harm them if they're incorrect.

Maya: *The very last thing that you said in the TED talk was a question, 'Do we want artificial intelligence to affect society as it is today, or as an ideal equitable society of tomorrow?' What do you think the answer to that question is?*

Robin: It needs to reflect an equitable society of tomorrow, because we always need to be striving to be better than we are, and to solve for some of our injustices and problems. If we just took the world today as it is when we know that we have an unjust world right now, then, we're just going to perpetuate that. I believe that we need to create software and artificial intelligence now, that will help us get to a just world.

Maya: *As a person who has studied and learned a ton about biases, are you socially aware of when you are using bias or when other people are biased; what is an example of people being unintentionally and intentionally biased?*

Robin: I hope that I'm becoming increasingly aware of my own biases. However, what worries me is that I know there are biases that I have which I can't identify, and that's very common for most humans. Just like how you can't do two math problems in your head at once, you can't really see all of your own biases. The important thing to do is to gather people around you that are different than you and to rely on them to check in with you because it's much easier to see bias in other people than it is in ourselves. If we're trying to bring in one other person to your team that's going to build a robot, for example, we need to make sure to not just rely on your own instinct about whether this one girl is going to be the one person that you want to bring onto the team because you might be suffering from something called 'like me' bias. We all have this.

It's the easiest thing to bring somebody on that's most like you, because that's who you are comfortable with. If you have a diverse group of friends and you say to them, "Well, I felt like Sonia was the best person to bring on, what do you all think?" Then you're going to get a varied opinion, and together as a team, you'll be able to come up with a decision that won't rely just on you in case some of your biases are getting in the way. So, one of the important things that I'm trying to do now is really check my gut and when I have a strong feeling about something, or I have a first impression. The goal is to just stop, slow down a little bit, ask people around me, does this seem like the right decision or am I just doing that because it's what my gut is telling me to do? And we know that your gut is not always dependable.

Maya: *If you have to set up a governmental, regulatory body for AI, how would you do it? Are other countries are doing this better?*

Robin: I know that we're looking into it, Microsoft and IBM are dedicating a lot of time and money to this. I don't know if other countries are working on it though, but I would think that they are. I don't actually know how I would set it up. That's not really within my skill set, but I would say that it should be set up with people who aren't just coding, developing, and creating the AI; it should also include end users and people who might be able to detect and understand the impact that some of the bias in AI has on the world and our society. So, I would make sure that this governing body was divided to have a very diverse group.

Maya: *Have you noticed bias with voice assistance, such as Cortana, Alexa or Siri?*

Robin: I can't give you an exact example, but the fact that all of them are female voices in itself, is a little bit biased. This assumption that she's an assistant and therefore she's a woman—I think that's interesting. I'm sure there's some interesting biases, but I can't bring it up to you on the spot. An interesting study for you to do is to start asking a lot of questions to Siri, Alexa, or Cortana and see what you might find.

Maya: *What leadership traits do you think you have to help advocate for girls in tech?*
Robin: I would say the leadership skill that I have is this ability to make documentary films that have my voice with people, with women who are trying to make their way in a male dominated world. I am not as afraid as I used to be looking out and seeing what's on my mind; confidence is a really important thing, even if we don't always naturally have confidence. Personally, I didn't go to film school or had a lot of experience in filmmaking before I jumped into it. Just having confidence through finding the right help, asking a lot of questions, admitting that you don't always know the right answer to something and you're working really hard, will certainly enable you to be successful in things you endeavor. If you're not originally successful, then you need to look at that as a learning opportunity as well.

Maya: *How early do you think we should start having STEM education introduced in schools so that it becomes part of a core curriculum especially for girls?*
Robin: We need to start as early as possible. I mean, I really believe that we should start in preschool and kindergarten. And there are a lot of games out there that teach the fundamentals

of logic and coding. So, there's a lot of really great stuff to do. There are a lot of great products out there that are designed for young people, men, women, girls, and boys. But I don't think it's ever too early to start. I think we can start at nursery school and we should be talking to all kids.

Maya: *What advice would you have for young girls?*
Robin: Find a mentor, know that it can be a man or a woman, but find somebody that you admire and ask for their support. Believe that you can do anything in the world, because you can, you really can, you can do anything you put your mind to, you just have to work really hard to get there. So, believe it. You deserve to be in the room, whatever room that is. Don't let failure discourage you, just keep pushing ahead. That's all we need to do.

Safra Catz

CEO, Oracle

Safra Catz has served as CEO of Oracle Corporation since 2014 and a member of the company's board of directors since 2001. She earned her bachelor's degree from the University of Pennsylvania and a J.D. from the University of Pennsylvania Law School. Catz was originally a banker before joining the Oracle Corporation. She was on Fortune's list as the 12th most powerful women in business and Forbes ranked her as the 16th most powerful female in business. She currently serves a director of The Walt Disney Company and previously served as a director of HSBC Holdings plc.

Maya: *What did you want to be when you were growing up?*
Safra: At one point, I wanted to be a scientist like my Dad. In college I took a business law class and so I decide to go to law school and be a corporate lawyer but as luck would have it, I didn't end up doing that either.

It's important that girls stay focused on building upon science and math fundamentals early on, and we want more women choosing the technical disciplines because they are both prepared to do so and because they believe it will advance their career options.

Maya: *You are CEO of one of the largest companies in the world. How does that feel? And what message does it send to young girls?*

Safra: I'm delighted that my career can help inspire and motivate the next generation of women leaders. I only wish there were more women in technology. Tech is about solving problems people don't realize they have yet. To solve problems, you want to include everyone. It's important that girls stay focused on building upon science and math fundamentals early on, and we want more women choosing the technical disciplines because they are both prepared to do so and because they believe it will advance their career options. I'm honored to be in a position that hopefully makes meaningful progress in this area.

Maya: *As the first female CEO of Oracle, have you made any changes to the company to make it more inclusive and provide more opportunities to women?*

Safra: Integrating the diverse perspectives of our employees into every aspect of business is what our business is all about. As part of our Diversity and Inclusion efforts, Oracle Women's Leadership (OWL) is one of the programs that I'm most proud of. The mission of OWL is to develop, engage, and empower current and future generations of Oracle women leaders to foster an inclusive and innovative workforce. OWL is open to all Oracle employees, engaging both men and women in this important work. Currently, there are 94 OWL communities in 46 countries.

Maya: *How can we get the world to pay more attention to STEM, especially girl's STEM education? How can we get more girls involved in technology at an early stage?*

Safra: It takes 25 years to build a computer engineer, not 25 hours. The computer sciences lose too many girls too early and, once lost, it's nearly impossible to get them back. At Oracle, we discovered that by the time people graduate, it's already too late. Even when entering college, it is too late. Through programs like Oracle Academy, Oracle Education Foundation, Oracle Giving and Volunteers, Oracle Women's Leadership (OWL), and Oracle Diversity and Inclusion, we offer education events across the globe including camps, codefests, workshops and conferences designed to encourage and inspire adolescent girls to become original thinkers and enterprising trailblazers. We've also developed curriculum around "wearable technology" that brings fashion and computing together, which makes it interesting and unleashes creativity.

Maya: *Why did you decide to build a high school at Oracle? How is it unique and different from other schools?*
Safra: We saw enormous potential in Design Tech High School (DTHS) innovative education model and knew the school needed a new home. Education is so important to us at Oracle, so the opportunity to partner with DTHS was perfect. We were able to help them, and it was the right thing to do. What's unique about Design Tech High School is that their education model is based on design thinking and students have the opportunity to work with Oracle Volunteers and the community to explore a variety of subjects directly from experts in those fields.

Maya: *There seems to be a big shift in technology with AI, Blockchain, Robotics, IoT, and other new technologies coming* *together. What changes do you anticipate in society as a result? How will automation impact jobs?*

Safra: AI is certainly going to involve an evolution in how people work, but that kind of disruption isn't new. AI can help free people from mundane tasks and allow them to do more interesting work. It's actually quite tremendous. A lot of technology used to be incredibly expensive and difficult to use, and now, the majority of consumers can use it. The potential is great. Though old jobs may disappear, new ones we haven't even imagined yet will be created.

Maya: *You have lot of experience in finance as well, how does that help you in your current job?*

Safra: Working in banking was one of the best decisions I ever made. Leaving banking was also one of the best decisions I ever made. I learned a lot while I was there and was fortunate to watch the expansion of the software industry when it was just beginning. That knowledge has helped me tremendously in making decisions to help transform Oracle's business.

Maya: *What leadership principles do you live by?*

Safra: The most important principle is courage. I've really learned about courage from Oracle's founder, Larry Ellison. Courage is about doing something new. A lot of people are comfortable doing things the old way — and they will constantly fight you. You have to have the courage of your convictions to make important change happens. Equally important is to be flexible and understand that continuing to do what made you successful in the past may not be where your future is.

Maya: *What advice would you give to your younger self?*
Safra: Work hard and don't be afraid to ask questions. If you don't understand what is being said in a meeting or a classroom, chances are others don't understand either. Ask a question. Real solutions only come from constantly asking questions.

Squash Falconer

Mountaineer and Adventurer

Squash Falconer is a record-breaking mountaineer and adventurer. She was the first British woman to climb and paraglide off the summit of Mont Blanc after riding there on her motorbike from the UK. Throughout her life, Falconer has accomplished a lot including summiting the breathtaking Mt. Everest. She has done a 3000-mile journey on an ElliptiGO and set a new distance record for travel on an Elliptical bicycle. In 2018, Falconer gave birth to her daughter, Kit. When she's not out in the wild or busy climbing a mountain, Falconer enjoys the simple things in life — fresh air, a nice cup of tea, and her friends and family.

Maya: *You are a very accomplished mountaineer. What motivated you to get into this adventurous life?*
Squash: I grew up on a farm and I always loved being outdoors. Originally, I wanted to be a farmer. Then, I was kind of convinced at the school that perhaps I should try being a vet because that was a bit more becoming of a young lady. I realized later that I didn't actually want to become a farmer

and I wasn't really sure what I wanted to do. So, when I was 18, I came out to the French Alps ski season, I decided to take a gap year. I worked in the French Alps and I absolutely loved being in the mountains. That was when I met a group of friends who did a lot of endurance/adventure races, and who were really quite sporty. From there, I slowly started hearing more advanced and endurance sports. So, I started doing longer distance runs and getting outdoors more. It was a group of friends that were going to climb a mountain in South America. They were talking about that, and I was around at their house, and I said, I'd love to do something like that. They literally looked at me, and said, "Well Squash why don't you? You're fit enough physically." So, you know, I had a good team of people around me, and then I climbed my first mountain and it grew from that.

Maya: *Do you think you still would have been an adventurer and climber if you hadn't grown up on a farm?*
Squash: Growing up on a farm was great because I love being outdoors, but it wasn't until I actually came to the mountains, and met a group of people that were climbing mountains and doing that kind of thing, that I got into mountaineering. It opened my eyes and my friends inspired me to do that. Anybody can do that sort of thing. But sometimes you just have to see it. I've met people who are in their 30s, 40s, 50s even 60s, when they climbed their first mountain. Sometimes things aren't an option for people because they don't know, or they don't think they can. Or they don't have the right team of people around them. I think if I hadn't grown up on a farm, I could have still done this.

On that mountain, there was a guy on the team and when we got back down walking out from the base camp, he said to me, "Squash, you're strong enough to climb Everest." That was the first time I ever really believed it was an option for me, because up until that point, Mt. Everest was something other people did.

Maya: *Why did you decide to climb Mount Everest? Was it the hardest peak that you've climbed so far?*

Squash: I always thought that I would never climb Mt. Everest. I was never the little girl who wanted to climb Mt. Everest, it was just not my plan. Even when I started climbing bigger mountains in my early 20s, I didn't think I was ever going to do that. I wasn't interested. Then, I climbed another mountain which was one of the 8000-meter peaks. Honestly, I thought that would be the highest I'd go. On that mountain, there was a guy on the team and when we got back down walking out from the base camp, he said to me, "Squash, you're strong enough to climb Everest." That was the first time I ever really believed it was an option for me, because up until that point, Mt. Everest was something other people did. I didn't know how I'd do it and I didn't think it would be possible, but when he said to me that it was physically possible, I started thinking about it and then things started to happen. Once you decide on something, you don't always know how to get there, but when it's in your head it's amazing how things come together and appear in front of you. I started working towards my goal and it took me years to make it happen, but I did.

Maya: *Did you have any fears or setbacks that you had before climbing Everest?*

Squash: I had so many fears. I had fears way before I began climbing. In my head I was thinking, I shouldn't have said I was going to do this, how am I possibly going to do it. There were lots of mental and emotional fears. Then I did my training and like with a lot of things you always feel you should have done more, and you haven't done enough training or you're not strong enough. Since I was training hard, I didn't gain very much weight and I was worried that I was going to be skinny when I went to climb. When I set off for Everest, we were heading to the base camp in Kathmandu and I got really sick in a tent in Namche Bazar. I got sickness and diarrhea and lost even more weight. I felt terrible and really thought "This is it," we've not even got to the base camp and my expedition is over.

Then, the team leader said, "Listen, Squash, just calm down, get yourself better, make sure to eat, your body is strong enough, you'll recover and just take your time." He said you don't have to go at the same speed as the rest of the group, you can go slower, and so I just trusted that. I got myself better, and I reached base camp just fine. When I got to the base camp, it was the most intimidating place I've ever been to. It's not a flat, nice area, it's all set on rock and ice and surrounded by huge mountains. Every night avalanches are going off at the Khumbu Icefall — which is this big massive ice glacier that is constantly moving — and the avalanches sound like bombs going off around you. So, when I got to base camp, I was really scared. I was in this place that was so intimidating and to be honest the fear and the anxiety doesn't leave at all, it stays with you the whole time, but we made these small goals all the time. So, once we got to the base camp, we'd have a rest and our next goal was to reach Camp 1 and get back to the base camp. So, although it was hard, and we were nervous about it, we did it and that made us think of a reason that we can keep pushing, keep going, and take one day at a time.

Sometimes we were setting for the summit in the dark and at that time you're just so tired and exhausted because you've been on the mountain for months, and you still don't know if you're going to be able to do it, whether it's going to be good enough, if you're going to be physically strong enough, or if the altitudes will affect you. Even when you reach the top, there is still this lingering question — will I be able to get back down? So, it's not really until you're completely back down afterwards that the fear stops. I think it stays with you the whole time. But a great lesson that I learned from a dear friend of mine is that fear will not kill you, complacency will. Fear can be really positive because it allows you to focus your energy and really zone in on what you've got to do. Complacency is the thing that's a worry. If you're not careful or focused, then you could make a simple mistake and fall off and then something bad happens.

Maya: *How do you think adventure has shaped you as a person?*
Squash: I'm the person that I am today because of adventure. Everything about my personality, the way I live my life every day, is because of the adventures I have been able to undertake. It's been such a big part of my life. We learn a lot about people when you do these big expeditions, and you learn a huge amount about yourself. So, I realized who I was when I was under stress and pressure and that what kind of a person I wanted to be. I wanted to be a good reliable teammate. I wanted to be a person who could be honest enough about my own feelings. Every part of my personality is formed by the adventures that I've been on.

Maya: *How do you think teamwork and leadership traits play out for you as a climber?*
Squash: I learned a huge amount from my mountain expeditions. Teamwork is so important. Although we achieve

things as solo individuals, we never really do anything on our own. We always have people helping us, supporting and guiding us, and holding us back if we need to be held. On the mountain, something I noticed that was really interesting was that different people have different strengths on different days. One day, you might be tired and need to lean on your team for support so they can feed you, give you water, help you physically or emotionally. On other days, you might be feeling strong and doing well. So, then you might be the one that is leading your team and giving the others strength. So, roles within the team shift and move, and we're all capable of being all those different parts. I never really thought of myself as a leader, but then I realized that leadership starts with yourself, we are all leaders, and we have to be because we have to make our own decisions. We make our own choices and sometimes that spills out onto others, because whether you are aware of it or not, people are watching your moves and learning from you, they're relying on you. It's not necessarily about standing up in front of everyone and telling everyone what to do. It's about being part of that team and leading by example.

Maya: *How did you come up with the idea of paragliding down mountains rather than climbing down them?*
Squash: When I was in my early 20s, I was working in the French Alps, and my friend was dating a paraglider pilot. Paragliding was so cool, I just loved it, but it wasn't something I knew how to do, or how to get into. Through this friend of mine, I got to meet a lot of paraglider pilots, and I used to talk to them and say, "You know, I'd love to do paragliding, I really want to get into it." One of the guys said to me, "Okay, well, I run a bed and breakfast and you can come there and work for

me during the summer and in exchange, I'll teach you how to fly." I thought this was an amazing opportunity, so I jumped on it. I went to work for him, and I learned how to fly that summer. When you learn to paraglide, you obviously jump off the side of big hills and mountains and I thought to myself, "This is so cool, I would love to fly off a really high mountain." Then when I decided to do the Mont Blanc trip, that's when I thought, "I've always wanted to climb Mont Blanc and I've always wanted to fly over a high mountain." I also always had this dream of riding a motorbike from my home in England, to the south of France. I thought I could combine all these things that I wanted to do into one amazing adventure, so I could ride my bike to the foot of Mont Blanc, then I could climb it and fly off the top. Everybody told me I was mad —like crazy mad! They thought I couldn't do it. This is another great piece of advice: to not always listen to what other people say and make your own decision. I decided I was going for it. And that's when I started flying.

Maya: *What pushed you to continue every step in all of your amazing adventures, whether it's biking throughout many countries, or climbing Mount Everest?*
Squash: I think it's a natural progression. As human beings, we have this desire to keep moving forward, or to keep going on. I love outdoor sports and adventures, the mountains, and paragliding. It's like I crave it. It's like people who go to the gym, they talk about having an addiction to go into the gym. If you go running, you want to do more, because it gives you a good feeling. I love the feeling of being fit, healthy and happy. It releases natural highs in your brain. I'm always chasing that because it makes me feel good and it doesn't even

have to be a big expedition — I try to work out every day. Before the workout, I don't want to do it and I find it quite difficult to motivate myself. Then I remember that afterwards, it's going to feel great. Since I've experienced those good feelings, I use them to keep me going and to keep pushing forward. I'm the first one to say it is really difficult to keep going, but I think when you've got a goal or a focus that may be very small or bigger goals to just keep going because of the feeling to want to be better and healthy.

Maya: *What's the next adventure for you?*
Squash: I am spending a lot of time focusing on turning all the different expeditions into a career. I suppose that's my ongoing talent. Since I climbed Mount Everest, I actually have gotten into debt to do the climb because I didn't raise enough money. So, I had to take out a loan and I promised myself when I got back I would either get a normal job to pay the money back or I would make a career out of what I was doing. It took me four years to pay the loan back, but I managed it. That was all through speaking, doing presentations, sharing my expeditions, working for outdoor companies and brands, doing projects like that. That has been my ongoing challenge. My climbing career is taking my speaking career to the next level. I'm really focused on that at the moment and of course, I always like to do an outdoor adventure.

Maya: *What advice would you have for your younger self?*
Squash: Stop worrying so much. When I was younger, I thought I had it figured out because I wanted to be a farmer and then I wanted to be a vet. Later, I reached this place where I didn't have a clue of what I wanted to do or where I wanted

to be. It was really difficult because I was always so focused and suddenly, I had all these options, but I didn't know what I wanted. I often say to people, sometimes you just have to work backwards and try lots of different things. Work out the things you don't want in order to figure out where you're going. I'd say to myself, relax, calm down, try lots of things. Don't worry about it. I'd also tell myself to believe in me a bit more. A lot of this was because I thought I wasn't good enough or I couldn't do it, and actually when I tried and pushed myself, I could do those things.

Maya: *What advice would you have for younger girls who want to follow your footsteps?*
Squash: One of the most important things I'd say to somebody is that with the right team of people around you as well as kindness and hard work, you'll be amazed at what you can achieve. Sometimes it takes years; these things don't just happen overnight. You know, I wanted to do things, but I didn't know how and it took me a long time to work it out, but once I did, it was a lot of fun. It's a long and difficult road sometimes, but don't give up. If you have a dream, my advice is to just don't give up. Keep pushing. Keep trying. And you will get there.

Tiffany Pham

CEO and Founder, Mogul

Tiffany Pham is CEO of Mogul, a company that provides tools to individuals & organizations to achieve optimal productivity & growth. A coder, she developed the first version of Mogul, now reaching millions of people across 196 countries and 30,470 cities. She is the bestselling author of YOU ARE A MOGUL and GIRL MOGUL. Pham was named one of Forbes' "30 Under 30" in media; in Business Insider "30 Most Important Women Under 30" in technology; in ELLE Magazine "30 Women Under 30 Who Are Changing the World;" Tribeca Film Festival "Innovation Award" Fellow, and SE "Top 100 Social Entrepreneur." She is a graduate of Yale & Harvard Business School.

Maya: *What do you think is the true definition of a mogul? How do you relate to it personally?*

Tiffany: A mogul to me is someone who is amazing at everything they wish to be. By that I mean, an amazing partner, mother, daughter, team player, or a team leader, whatever it is that you wish to be whether it's personally or professionally. So, to me, it was never about just being what was commonly seen as a successful businessperson. To me, a mogul is being the best that you could be across every aspect of your life, every facet of your being. How I relate to it is that I've known so many incredible women in my life, who are moguls, they are amazing business leaders, loved by the community because they are kind, warm, generous and authentic. My grandmother was exactly that. She was an amazing mogul herself, running businesses in Asia. I grew up, thereafter, thinking of her as a mogul.

Later on, when I went off to college, at Yale and Harvard Business School, I observed that a very few women were considered moguls. In fact, when I googled the word mogul, I would see that the first six pages of search results were successful businessmen. It wasn't until the seventh page that you would suddenly get to women's names. Today, if you google the word 'mogul', we are the number one search result. We have helped redefine that word mogul for the next generation of girls and women so that they know they can be moguls too.

Maya: *What was the key motivation to start this company?*
Tiffany: The motivation was actually to honor my grandmother, for all the incredible work that she had done. To ultimately help others in need with information and opportunities. So, ever since I was 14 years old, that's all I've ever worked towards. As I was applying to college at Yale, and Harvard Business School, every single time I would repeat this, that one day, I wish to create a company that would ultimately enable me to follow my grandmother's footsteps. I have tried to stay true to that. Actually, I forgot a fun fact for you, Maya, which is that my grandmother ran a newspaper

from Asia. So, that's why I wished to be like her by writing for the newspaper at my college. Thereafter, I worked on the building up the skills by taking a lot of different jobs that helped me in varying aspects of the business such business development, strategy, content creation, distribution, marketing, branding, product and technology.

I saw myself being written about in different newsletters and magazines one day. I started receiving letters from women asking for help and advice on how to get things started in their country and respective communities. So, I started to write back to every single letter I received and every single time young women would reply to my letter saying it changed their lives. I would go into details of steps needed to get their business going. That experience led me to the idea of Mogul.

I thought, what if we could create a platform where all of us could share our goals and dreams, I realized that I didn't have the money to hire engineers. Inspired by my grandmother, I taught myself how to code and built the site myself. I learned Ruby on Rails every single day at work in my three unusual jobs. I worked for CBS during the day. And at nights, I'd work with the Beijing government, and then further into my office with feature films and documentaries. But, then at night, at 3am, I will be done with everything. Then, I would just teach myself Ruby on Rails. After a couple of weeks of work, the first ugly version of the site was ready. I ended up sending out to all those women calling me online. Before I knew it, we ended up exploding to 10 million women within our first week, becoming the fastest growing platform for one another. Fast forward to today, now, we have become the largest ecosystem for women worldwide.

Maya: *What is the main idea that you want a reader to get out of your recent book on the subject?*

Tiffany: I wanted readers to be able to learn from my mistakes, learn the lessons I learned. I share every single part of the way I made mistakes, the lessons I learned, breaking it down so that they can apply it back in their lives right away. That, ultimately, is what I hope my readers take away from the book. From the feedback I have gotten, the book resonates well with women around the world.

Maya: *Were there any challenges or obstacles that you faced in your career as a female entrepreneur? How did you overcome them?*

Tiffany: Yes, as an entrepreneur, there were obstacles along the way. When I was first starting Mogul as a one-person team, I slept so little because I did everything from design, to the coding, to the selling, to the partnering, to the pitching, to the press and to the building of the community. I was doing everything, I loved it so much, it was so much fun looking back. And yet, all of a sudden, there were a million people coming to the platform and it was causing the site to crash. So I had to build a team, a world class team made up of incredible business leaders themselves.

I started having credible business leaders reach out to me and saying they would love to be a part. I brought them on board, and we started having good momentum. Now one of our challenges is to manage growth both in terms of infrastructure, the team that supports it and meeting the expectations of the community.

I started to write down every single one of my ideas during a meeting, during a class and that gave me the confidence to speak up. While I was shy and lacked confidence, I never wanted to have the feeling of regret. This motivated me to shed my introverted self when the situation demanded it.

Maya: *In one of the interviews that you did, you said that you were an introverted person. What advice would you give to girls who are shy but want to take on big challenges that involve working in teams*

Tiffany: I am an introvert and I am a shy person. So, when I was speaking publicly, I found myself hesitating all the time. I tried to overcome that through writing. I started to write down every single one of my ideas during a meeting, during a class and that gave me the confidence to speak up. While I was shy and lacked confidence, I never wanted to have the feeling of regret. This motivated me to shed my introverted self when the situation demanded it.

Maya: *So, how do you think we can encourage more girls to pursue STEM careers?*

Tiffany: There are two ways in which to encourage girls in STEM. First, developing a mindset that failure is okay, and that it's okay to not be perfect. At the beginning, it's all about rapidly, putting yourself out there, taking action, trying and then perfecting over time. I think I realized, that girls are oftentimes encouraged to be perfect, to be pretty, to be smart. But, in reality, we should be encouraging all boys and girls equally to be brave and courageous and to go out there and trying and taking action. I got that from my father growing up as a young girl. He was always encouraging me to try to do things. So, mindset is number one. Number two is to ultimately have them see and meet more role models. That helps in seeing their full potential.

Maya: *Have you had any great mentors? What is the best advice that you've gotten?*

Tiffany: Yes, I've had so many great mentors. I regard my supervisors as my mentors, I regard my peers to be mentors, I regard direct reports to be mentors. To be honest, I see anyone from whom I can learn to be a mentor. However, people who taught me the most are of course, my parents, especially my father. He is always looking to teach me, coach me to be better and not be afraid of trying out new things. He taught me to be kind and generous and be in the service of others.

Additionally, I have benefitted from the guidance of the heads of NPR, MTV, McGraw Hill Education, Diane Von Furstenberg, Gary Banner, and Suzie Orman. These are all incredible icons, public figures and leaders who continue to support me with their invaluable advice. I am very grateful to them.

Maya: *How do you manage your personal life with your career?*
Tiffany: I love integrating my personal and professional lives into one. I believe in work-life integration. Otherwise, I don't necessarily believe in the classical work-life balance concept. I believe in work-life integration. Because I bring it all into one, I believe in being authentically myself across both as I bring in my family, my sons, my loved ones across both dimensions of my life.

Maya: *There's been a lot of talk on automation, AI, and robotics. How do you think that all this will impact society and future jobs? And do you think society is ready for this big change?*
Tiffany: Well, I think AI and robotics are going to have a lot of positive impact on the world. I think that they're going to automate a lot of parts of the existing jobs. Ideally, this will

bring more ROI, especially in areas that don't require human touch. I think Emotional Intelligence (EQ) will be equally important going forward. So, we can have robots focus on areas that are repetitive and humans address the areas that require love, emotion, and EQ.

Maya: *You have had a pretty successful career. What is the next big thing for you?*

Tiffany: Well, the next big thing for us is our new Mogul app. I hope you download it and try it out. It's amazing. When I look back upon my life, I realized that one of the most powerful things I ever did was to develop a system in which I became extremely efficient and productive in my life. I ended up developing a system whereby I was able to break down the to-do's I had each day and thus create smaller milestones that address my short-term and long-term goals. The app is revolutionary in this area, and it enables our community to be there alongside you as well provide ongoing mentorship, coaching and support.

I want to continue to use our platform to enable billions of women around the world to lead a productive and satisfying life. That's what keeps me motivated every day.

Image References:

1. https://www.zimbio.com/photos/Ada+E.+Yonath/Nobel+Prize+Award+Ceremony+2009/9HdvnXUnuSs
2. https://www.bizjournals.com/atlanta/news/2017/09/06/q-a-nasdaq-ceo-adena-friedman-talks-705m-evestment.html
3. https://trueventures.com/team/ann-crady-weiss/
4. https://www.washington.edu/president/biography/
5. https://www.cnbc.com/2018/03/20/arianna-huffington-avoids-3-bad-habits-that-can-tank-your-success.html
6. https://en.wikipedia.org/wiki/Ashley_Parker
7. https://workingcapitalreview.com/2018/10/comstock-bringing-imagination-to-business/
8. https://www.britannica.com/biography/Ellen-Ochoa
9. https://www.refinery29.com/en-us/2018/02/190583/emily-chang-brotopia-interview
10. https://www.finsmes.com/2019/10/peterson-ventures-adds-ilana-stern-as-general-partner.html
11. https://www.nowtolove.co.nz/lifestyle/career/how-jacinda-ardern-is-managing-her-pregnancy-on-top-of-her-role-as-prime-minister-of-nz-36800
12. https://time.com/5131942/janet-yellen-fed-brookings/
13. https://www.spokesman.com/stories/2017/nov/28/jenny-durkan-sworn-in-as-seattles-first-female-may/

14. https://physicsworld.com/a/jocelyn-bell-burnell-reveals-the-motivations-behind-her-new-3m-graduate-student-fund/

15. https://listen.sdpb.org/post/jody-williams-land-mines-and-1st-amendment

16. https://www.forbes.com/sites/stevenbertoni/2017/12/12/cnn-reporter-laurie-segall-dives-into-techs-dark-side/#2382f54b529c

17. https://en.as.com/en/2019/02/10/other_sports/1549799495_143085.html

18. https://www.britannica.com/biography/Maria-Cantwell

19. https://www.issaquahwa.gov/528/Mary-Lou-Pauly-Mayor

20. https://en.wikipedia.org/wiki/Patty_Murray

21. https://commons.wikimedia.org/wiki/File:Pramila_Jayapal_115th_Congress_photo.jpg

22. https://www.tedxmarin.org/speaker/robin-hauser/

23. https://www.flickr.com/photos/mikereys/2902616504/

24. https://www.squashfalconer.com/

25. https://www.forbes.com/sites/geekgirlrising/2017/07/18/how-this-female-founder-took-on-sexism-and-raised-millions/#4d7ae12b1dfe

CPSIA information can be obtained
at www.ICGtesting.com
Printed in the USA
BVHW010255290121
599078BV00014B/270